Phenomenal Digital Photo Tricks

friendsof

BREAK YOUR CREATIVE BOUNDARIES

99 Phenomenal Digital Photo Tricks

© 2003 friends of ED

First Printed February 2003

Published by friends of ED

Arden House, 1102 Warwick Road,
Acocks Green, Birmingham.
B27 6BH.

Printed in USA

Credits

Authors
Kevin Francis
Jim Hannah
Chris Matterface
Crystal Waters
Simon Wheatley
Liz Wheatley
Dave Yates

Commissioning Editor
Jim Hannah

Project Manager
Richard Harrison

Technical Editors
Libby Hayward,
Adam Juniper

Graphic Editor
Katy Freer

Author Agent
Chris Matterface

Proof Readers
Simon Collins
Joanne Crichton

Managing Editor
Chris Hindley

Contents

Each chapter contains three phenomenal digital photo tricks!

99 Phenomenal Digital Photo Tricks

We've all seen funny pictures — they land in your email inbox every day — sometimes they even make the newspapers. Now it's time for you to join in the fun!

These 99 Phenomenal Digital Photo Tricks will amaze and delight your friends and family. What is more, we have provided step-by-step explanations in the five most popular pieces of image editing software, so you know exactly what's going on!

Whether you're using **Photoshop Elements**, **Photoshop**, **Paint Shop Pro**, **PhotoImpact** or **Picture It!** there's a wealth of fun and information here for you. All you need is one of these pieces of software, a minute or three, and the rest is up to your imagination!

Where do I get pictures?

If you want to get going on a few ideas, we've provided a selection of images for you to use online. Go to www.friendsofed.com/99 and have a play — some of the images are from this book, and some are completely new, so you can have fresh ideas about them!

Prizes!

At www.friendsofed.com/99 you can compare your images to those of other readers! We'd be delighted if you'd send us your best efforts, and we will host a gallery of the best pictures we receive. Every month we will be giving prizes to the best images, and we will regularly run public votes to see which you think is the best!

Here's an opportunity to win access to the complete friends of ED photo-editing and digital graphics library, with tuition and tips from some of the world's most highly rated artists and technicians. Digital Photography and photo-editing is a huge field with so many routes to take on your own preferred learning journey. At friends of ED we can provide you with peer-reviewed resources at every level of your artistic progression, plus a constant supply of ideas to help you break your own creative boundaries.

Why not get involved, and pick up a few handy hints and tips along the way?

You will find links on the site to a whole host of materials, including friends of ED's other photo editing titles, including **Digital Photography with Photoshop Elements**, **Photoshop Elements 2 Zero to Hero**, **Photoshop Elements 2 Most Wanted** and **Pro Photo Techniques**.

Software and Tools

There are so many pieces of Digital Imaging software – you'd never get this book through your front door if we included them all!

We have included instructions for the five most popular picture editing software packages – **Adobe Photoshop** and **Adobe Photoshop Elements**, **Jasc Paint Shop Pro**, **Ulead PhotoImpact** and **Microsoft Picture It!** They are represented by the following icons:

 Photoshop/Photoshop Elements

Paint Shop Pro

 PhotoImpact

Picture It!

If you don't have any of these pieces of software, don't worry! Free trial versions of the latest are available for download – they'll last only 30 days, but you'll certainly be able to case out the possibilities of each:

Photoshop/Photoshop Elements: http://www.adobe.com/products/tryadobe/
Paint Shop Pro: http://www.jasc.com/download_4.asp
PhotoImpact: http://www.ulead.com/pi/trial.htm

How do I use the software?

All the instructions are included for all the software, but if you have any queries, you can refer to our handy quick reference section below. Simply look for the tool, and you will find simple instructions and an overview of the comparable tools in each piece of software.

By the way, if you're looking to upgrade your software, this book provides an excellent opportunity to see what differentiates the competition!

Support

Like all friends of ED books, 99 Phenomenal Digital Photo Tricks is backed by fast, free and friendly technical support. If you have any problems with the work, one of our editors will be delighted to help you out. Simply mail support@friendsofed.com with your query, and we will get back to you as quickly as we can!

Introducing the Tools

The tricks in this book utilize some staple tools in photo-editing, and often each of the pieces of software has its own variation of the same tool. This is your guide to those tools and what to do with them!

Tool Instructions	Photoshop/ Photoshop Elements	Paint Shop Pro	PhotoImpact	Picture It!
Move Tool – *This tool enables you to move objects or selections around.*				
Marquee Tool – *Click and drag to select a rectangle of your image. Feathering – to soften the edges of the selection, set the feathering value to a few pixels.*				**Create a Cutout** How do you want to cut out an object from your picture? With the Edge Finder / By tracing an area on my own / By color selection / With a cookie cutter shape / Help — Follow the Crop or Rotate path and use a cookie cutter shape.
Lasso Tool – *the free-hand version of the Marquee Tool. Simply click and draw the selection you want to make. Feathering – to soften the edges of the selection, set the feathering value to a few pixels.*	Lasso Tool	Freehand	Lasso Tool	**Create a Cutout** How do you want to cut out an object from your picture? With the Edge Finder / By tracing an area on my own / By color selection — Follow the Crop or Rotate path and opt to trace your own area.

Tool Instructions	Photoshop/ Photoshop Elements	Paint Shop Pro	PhotoImpact	Picture It!
Magic Wand Tool – *selects all instances of a particular color – very handy for selecting flat blue sky against a wavy landscape.*	Click to make a selection. Use the top menu to alter sensitivity.	Click to make a selection. Use the Tool Options dialog to alter sensitivity.	Click and hold on the standard selection tool to find! Click to make a selection. Use the the top menu to alter sensitivity.	No equivalent tool.
Brush – *this is your standard click and drag tool, imitating a paintbrush. Size, shape and opacity.*				Follow the Effects > Freehand painting path.
Eraser – *this tool acts like the Brush, but erases whatever you've done. Size, shape and opacity.*			Rather than having a single eraser, each tool has an eraser toggle in it. Click it to erase instead of paint!	You'll find the Eraser among the Paint tools options in the Freehand painting window.
Clone Stamp – *This popular tool makes retouching easy. Simply nominate the area of your picture you want to copy, and then paint it in elsewhere on the canvas! Size, shape and opacity.*	Alt-click to nominate, then click and drag to paint	Right-click to nominate, then click and drag to paint.	Shift-click to nominate, then click and drag to paint.	No equivalent tool, although there are several automatic retouching tools under the Touchup menu.

Tool Instructions	Photoshop/ Photoshop Elements	Paint Shop Pro	PhotoImpact	Picture It!
Paint Bucket – *This acts like a big bucket of paint. Simply click to fill large areas of your picture.*				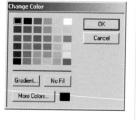 Click through Format > Shape or Line > Fill Color.
Gradient Tool – *This is related to the Fill tool, and creates a smooth gradient between two or more colors. The tool can provide linear gradients, circular (radial) gradients, plus selected other sorts.*	 Gradient Tool	 Gradient tool – reveal it by clicking on the Styles button.	 Gradient fill tool – reveal it by clicking and holding on the Bucket Fill tool icon.	Click the Gradient button in the Fill Color window.
Layer Palette – *This palette shows you the number of Layers you have in your image. You can drag layers around in it, and you can merge whichever layers you like. Layer opacity can be customized.*			 Layer Manager can be toggled on/off by pressing the Layer Manager button	 The Stack

Tool Instructions	Photoshop/ Photoshop Elements	Paint Shop Pro	PhotoImpact	Picture It!
Layer Blending Modes – *alter the layer blending mode to make the layers respond differently to one another.*	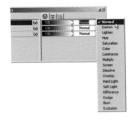		PhotoImpact does not do all layer blending.	Picture It! Does not do any layer blending.
Merging Layers – *sometimes in this book you are required to merge layers together.*	 To merge all the layers, click through Layers > Flatten Image. To merge selected layers, first click in the Link box and then click through Layers > Merge Linked.	 Click through Layers > Merge > Merge Visible. If you want to keep any layer unmerged, simply make it invisible first by clicking on the Layer Visibility toggle!	 Click through Object > Merge.	You cannot merge layers in Picture It!, but you can group objects on different layers by clicking through Edit > Group.
Type Tool – *This enables you to type text into your image.*	 Simply click and type. Adjust the font format in the top menu bar.	 Click, and enter your type and formatting into the dialog. To edit, double click your typing to reopen the dialog.	 Simply click and type. Adjust the font format in the top menu bar.	 Simply click and type. Adjust the font format in the top menu bar.

Tool Instructions	Photoshop/ Photoshop Elements	Paint Shop Pro	PhotoImpact	Picture It!
Hue/Saturation – *This dialog enables you to alter the hue, saturation and brightness of an image*		Find by typing Shift + H	Find by typing Ctrl + E.	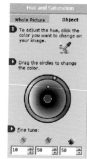Touch Up > Hue/Saturation.
Filters – *These are ready-made effects that the software carries. You can easily apply them to any image. Each filter has a different self-explanatory dialog.*	Click Filter, and you will be given a drop-down box with all the different kind of filters.	Click Effects, and you will be given a drop-down box of different effects.	Click Effect and you will be given a dropdown window of different effects.	Click Effects and you will be given a dropdown window of different effects.
Layer styles – *these apply drop-shadows, bevels, and glows to selected layer.*	Find the layer styles tab in the top menu.			

Death Valley

Trick 1: Vacuuming Death Valley

You will need:

- Someone vacuuming.
- An unlikely landscape to vacuum.

To complete the effect:

1. In our vacuuming example, the first thing we need to do is adjust the vibrant red tones in the jumper. We'll need to select the jumper so that we can make an adjustment without affecting the rest of the picture. The best way to do this is to zoom in so the jumper fills your screen. Use a lasso tool to select around it.

(If you are using Picture It! then you can make a selection by going to Format > Create a Cutout and then opt to trace the area yourself). Once you've got a selection, take a minute to use the 'add to' and 'subtract from' lasso modes to make sure everything is neatly enclosed in the selection. Save the selection to its own separate layer.

2. With the jumper layer selected, bring up the Hue/Saturation dialog box (In Photoshop Elements it's CTRL/⌘+U, in Paint Shop Pro SHIFT+H, PhotoImpact CTRL/⌘+E, and in Picture It! you need to go to Touch Up > Hue/Saturation). Decrease the Saturation a little (maybe –5) and decrease the lightness a little (maybe –10) – it's not a precise art, so see what looks right.

3. To increase the definition on the background layer use the Auto Contrast command, which you'll find under the same menu as the Hue/Saturation command that we just used. Once you're happy with the look, merge the layers. (In Picture It! you can do this by SHIFT-clicking the appropriate layers in the Stack and then going to Edit > Group).

4. Save your work so far, then (without closing the original document) open your landscape and immediately save it under a new name. Then switch back to your original document.

5. Using the Lasso or Magnetic Lasso tool, create a selection around the person and vacuum cleaner. Again 'add to' and 'subtract from' your selection to create the right shape.

6. When you've finished creating your selection use the Feather command (CTRL/⌘+ALT+D in Photoshop Elements) to soften the edges by one or two pixels. This will ensure that we don't have a harsh edge to our image, which would be unnatural in a hot desert with heat haze.

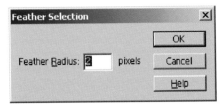

7. With the object still selected, select Copy (CTRL/⌘+C), then switch to the target document and Paste (CTRL/⌘+V). If you like, give the new layer an appropriate name. You can now use the Move tool to position your subject.

8. Create a new layer, between the background and your subject. Set its opacity down, then use a soft brush tool to paint on the shadow. PhotoImpact does not allow you to create new layers, so you will need to paint your shadow directly onto your background layer. By contrast Picture It! will create your new layer automatically when you select the Paintbrush option (Effect > Paintbrush > Freehand). Err on

the side of too big because we can always erase unwanted extra. In Photoshop, you can use the Multiply Blending Mode for a more realistic effect.

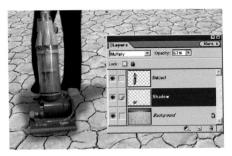

9. Using the Polygonal Lasso tool create a straight edged selection running out in front of the vacuum cleaner. It should be as wide as the front of the vacuum cleaner on that end, and slightly wider at the front (to create a subtle sense of perspective) running right to the edge of the picture. Feather the selection by about 5 pixels. (If you have problems creating the new selection in PhotoImpact then try merging the other objects).

10. When you are happy with your selection, copy it as a new layer below the Shadow layer. (Layer > New Layer > Via Copy in Photoshop). Then use the Brightness/Contrast (or whatever you consider appropriate) tool to lighten the vacuumed path. A light Gaussian Blur will also make the surface look a little cleaner.

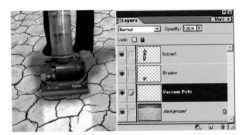

The Badwater point of Death Valley is the lowest point in the Western Hemisphere, 282ft below sea level.

There are over 900 different species of plants in Death Valley.

The floor of Death Valley was once a lake!

In 2001, there were 153 consecutive days with temperatures above 100 degrees!

Trick 2: Death Valley filling in the cracks

You will need:
- One photo of Death Valley
- One photo of a diligent worker with a filling knife

To complete the effect:
- Copy and paste in the diligent worker and add a shadow, as per the instructions in the main effect.
- If you've got Photoshop then filling in the layers couldn't be easier. Create a new layer, select the Clone Stamp tool (and select Use All Layers), and carefully color the cracks back in. Unfortunately there is not Clone Stamp tool in Picture It!, but you can create a similar effect by going to Touch Up > Remove Scratches.
- If you use the tool carelessly, you'll get a "banding" effect, which can actually work to our advantage here and make the diligent worker look a little more human.

Trick 3: Death Valley shadows

You will need:
- One photo of Death Valley
- A picture with an appropriate shadow or shape

To complete the effect:
- Use the Lasso tool to select the shadow shape, copy this selection.
- Copy and paste the selection into the Death Valley image.
- Apply a strong Gaussian Blur of about 10 pixels to make the edges fuzzy.
- Now you've got your basic shadow, duplicate the layer.
- Set the blending mode of the lower shadow's layer to Overlay.
- Set the opacity of both layers to 50%.

The Royal Albert Hall

Trick 4: London Flooded

You will need:

- One picture of Royal Albert Hall

To complete the effect:

1. Make a copy of the Albert Hall background layer – our new layer will have our reflection on it. Increase the height of the image to 22cm, so that blank space appears beneath (in Photoshop, this is the Image > Canvas Size command, in Photo Impact Format > Expand Canvas).

2. Use the Rectangular Marquee tool to create a selection across the width of the image, starting at the top and ending just below the red London bus' wheel arches. Flip the selection vertically (Image > Rotate > Flip Selection Vertically in Photoshop) and move it down so the top is level with just under the wheel arches of the red London bus.

3. The street looks slightly awkward, so crop it off to concentrate the image on the Royal Albert Hall.

4. Use a ripple filter to give the reflection layer a ripple effect. In Photoshop, this is Filters > Distort > Ripple. In Paint Shop Pro a similar effect can be found under Effects > Geometric Effects > Ripple, but it will ripple around a center – use a target that might make ripples. In Picture It there is no ripple effect, but you can create a watery effect by applying a strong blur, Touchup > Sharpen or Blur, and then add a watercolor effect.

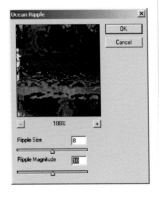

5. Duplicate the reflection layer and blur the copy with a strong Gaussian Blur – around 10 pixels.

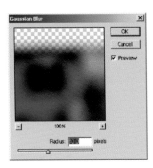

6. Still on the reflection layer, reduce the color saturation using the Hue/Saturation dialog box.

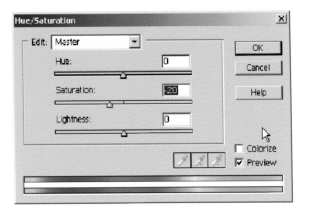

7. Place the blurred reflection layer beneath the reflection layer and set the reflection's opacity to 50%.

8. On the reflection layer, create a straight edged selection around the reflection of the white stripes on the green bus using the "Polygonal Lasso" tool. Use the "feather" command in the "select" menu to feather the selection by 5 pixels.

9. Using the Free Transform tool, rotate the selected stripes so they are roughly parallel with the bus above. The shortcut is CTRL/⌘+T in Photoshop, and CTRL+R in Paint Shop Pro.

10. If you like, soften the edge of the water at the top in the background by selecting all of the blank pixels in the reflection layers, applying a 10 pixel feather then clicking delete. Repeat for both reflection layers.

The Royal Albert Hall is named after Queen Victoria's husband, and was opened in the same year as the Albert memorial.

The Hall was opened on 29th March 1871 by the grieving Queen herself.

The volume of the auditorium is 3.5 million cubic feet!

Alfred Hitchcock staged two assassination attempts in the Hall, in two different films, both called *The Man Who Knew Too Much*, over 20 years apart.

Trick 5:
Adding extra floors to the Royal Albert Hall

You will need:

- One picture of the Royal Albert Hall or a suitable substitute.

To complete the effect:

- Copy and paste portions of the Albert Hall into new layers. Each portion should be selected from the bottom of the shadow cast by the balcony with the balustrades up to the top of the picture. Do this twice, so you have two new layers.
- Position the first layer so that the shadow of the bottom of its balcony is just below the frieze. Repeat this with the second layer, so that its shadow is just below the frieze of the first layer. Call one layer "balcony 1" and the second "balcony 2".
- Carefully erase any parts of the layer that appear in the wrong place.
- If you are brave enough to tackle the doorway, then it's more of the same.
- Extend the arched window on the right-hand wall of the doorway so that it covers the full height of the wall. Simply copy and paste new layers (called window 1 and 2) to create the extra height, then erase away until it looks right.

Trick 6:
A giant hand playing with the London bus

You will need:

- An image of London featuring a famous red London bus.
- A picture of an arm with the hand in an appropriate position.

To complete the effect:

- Use the Lasso tool to cut the arm using feathering. You may wish to take a shot of the arm especially with a digital camera to get the position of the hand just right.
- Place it and drag it into position using the move tool.
- Duplicate the arm layer, then move the lower layer a little way behind (this will form our shadow).
- Using the Levels or Brightness/Contrast command, adjust the arm image until the entire arm appears black (in Levels this is achieved by dragging the left-hand slider to the right).
- Apply a strong blur to the shadow layer, and adjust the layers opacity.
- Erase some areas of the shadow (or paint more in using a black brush) to give the impression of the shadow being cast closer to the fingers where they're touching the bus.
- Finally, create a new topmost layer with a graduated fill from black to transparent in the top right hand corner to give the impression of something more than the arm out of shot.
- Reduce the opacity of this layer to around 20%.

Old Faithful

Trick 7: Old Faithful blowing bubbles

You will need:

- An image of Old Faithful.

To complete the effect:

1. Duplicate the background. Keep the old background, but make it invisible.

2. Drag a freehand Lasso around the sky and over the rise and fall of the horizon; use this to delete the sky. Check you've not cut off any features from the skyline. It's up to you how precise you are, but remember this needs to look good.

3. Create a new, blank layer beneath the horizon layer. Now, temporarily turn on the visibility of the original background layer, and use the Eyedropper tool to sample colors for your new sky.

4. To make a convincing sky we're going to create a gradient. You will find the Gradient tool on the Tool Options bar in Photoshop, from the Styles preview button beneath the color palette in Paint shop Pro, and from the Color panel in PhotoImpact. Select the Edit option to create a custom gradient fading from the dark to colors of the original sky.

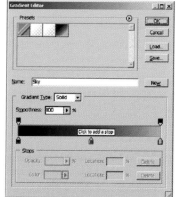

5. Check your colors and gradient; you may want to adjust them a little. Once you've got the gradient set up, select the 'sky gradient' layer and drag your gradient tool between the top left and bottom right (or in Paint Shop Pro remember to set the angle when you edit the gradient).

6. Use the clone tool to clone over the plume from the gray clay ground and tree line to either side.

7. Now we've got rid of the original feature, we can add our bubbles. The bubbles will be composed of three or four semi-transparent layers:

- A fish eye effect on the background behind the bubble
- A white radial gradient shine
- A white, slightly blurred outline
- A rainbow soap film

All these layers will be distorted slightly to add reality. You'll be using the three gradients repeatedly so remember to save them to save time.

8. Make a circular selection where you want your bubble, (in Photoshop and Paint Shop Pro now place this selection on its own layer). Use the Spherize filter or effect to create a fish eye effect on your circular selection. In PhotoImpact this filter is found under Effect > 3D > Sphere).

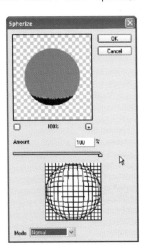

9. On a new layer above, but with the same selected area, create a radial gradient from 100% opaque white (on the edge) to 100% transparent white (in the centre.)

10. On yet another new layer above, but still with the same selected area, use the default or your own rainbow gradient tool from just past one edge of the selection to just past the opposite edge.

11. Reduce the opacity of your bubble layers

Repeat your bubble as many times and at as many different sizes as you like. Experiment with different shape bubbles to see what effects you can create.

It's actually not the oldest, nor the biggest nor the most regular geyser in Yellowstone.

It's in Yellowstone National Park, in Wyoming.

Length of eruptions are from 90 seconds to 5 minutes.

Up to 8,400 gallons of boiling water shoot some 150 feet skyward roughly every 76 minutes.

Trick 8: Old Faithful Flying Cork

You will need:

- One photo of Old Faithful with the background removed (see the first part of the main effect in this chapter).
- One photo of a champagne cork - You don't *have* to use champagne... but it's a good excuse.

To complete the effect:

- Cut out the cork from the original and place over the steam.
- Duplicate the cork layer, and apply a motion blur to the higher of the two.
- Use the eraser tool, with soft edges, to delete the upper areas of the blurred cork, so that the blur seems only to form a tail.
- Then merge the cork layers and even more gently erase the trailing edge of the cork so that it appears to be emerging from the vapor.
- If you like, clone some clouds over the cork with a low opacity brush.

Trick 9: Old Faithful Smoking

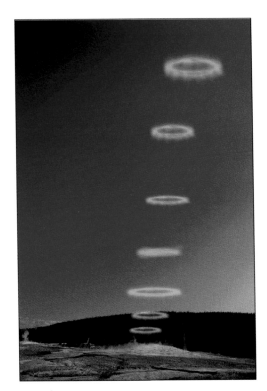

You will need:

- One photo of Old Faithful.

To complete the effect:

- Remove the smoke stack, as in Trick #7.
- Create a feathered elliptical selection to act as an edge for each of your rings.
- Use a soft edged brush at a low opacity to draw your smoke rings. (In Photoshop or Photoshop Elements, you can take advantage of the Scatter option from the More Options menu to the right of Tool Options bar).
- Create the smoke rings one at a time, making them wider the further they are from the "source".
- Use a motion blur set to 10 pixels in a horizontal direction on all the smoke ring layers.
- Play with the opacity and positioning of the smoke ring layers to finish the effect.

The Parthenon

Trick 10: Imprisoned in Acropolis

You will need:

- Someone in a trapped pose.
- A suitably restricting monument, Greek architecture is the way to go here.

To complete the effect:

1. Carefully run the lasso around the figure leaving a bit spare round the edges on difficult areas like the fluffy hair at the top.

2. Open your target monument and duplicate the background layer, copy your selected area onto it as a new layer. Scale if necessary so the fingers seem appropriately positioned.

3. If masking is available to you then this is probably the best way to complete the next step. Select Mask mode and make sure you have the Parthenon layer selected. Now use black paint to cover the prisoner's hands and the areas between the pillars where his face and body would show through. When you come out of mask mode, you will see that the prisoner will appear from behind his bars.

4. Masking is not available in some programs, including Photoshop Elements, so here is a workaround: Place the duplicate background layer above the prisoner layer. Reduce the opacity temporarily so we can see what we are doing.

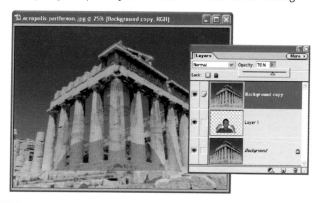

5. Select the pixels, with a very minor feather, in the gaps between pillars on the top layer and delete them (you could also do this using the Eraser tool).

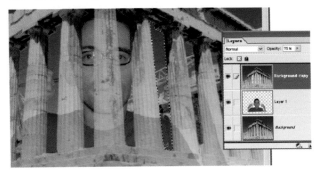

6. Switch to the layer beneath – the prisoner – and carefully select the hands. With a small feather (say 1 pixel) select the area where the hand will grip the pillar (don't worry if you go a bit over at either side, but be close at the top and bottom).

7. With that area selected, switch to the top layer and delete the pixels above it. The hand should now be solidly visible.

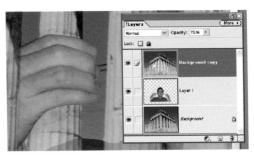

In Picture It! the best way to achieve this effect is by placing the prisoner layer above the monument, then making a cutout around the areas of the prisoner that need to be concealed by the pillars, and selecting the opposite area, delete the layer which contains the prisoner image intact, and finally you should be left with the hapless prisoner appearing from behind his bars.

8. Still working on the top layer, use the Burn tool (Photoshop) to darken the area beneath where the hand is to give an impression of shadow. Repeat these steps for the opposite hand. If you don't have a Burn tool then use a soft light brush at low opacity with colors that are slightly darker than the pillar to create a shadow effect.

9. Add any shadow effects you like to the layer beneath also.

10. Reset the opacity of the top layer to 100% so the 'ghost' effect disappears and our chap appears to be behind bars.

11. Finally, you can create a knuckle effect by erasing more of the top layer where the knuckles should be. Then shade the trapped person layer with the Burn tool.

The Acropolis is in Athens, Greece, and was walled before the 6th century BC.

Although the Acropolis was battered by the Persians in 480 BC, remains still stand.

Like many monuments, the Acropolis has suffered severely from abortive repair attempts.

Trick 11: Underwater Antiquity

Trick 12: Stripy Acropolis

You will need:

- One picture of an ancient ruin.
- A background shot taken underwater.

To complete this effect:

- Open your underwater image.
- Add a copy of your Parthenon (or equivalent) in the layer above.
- Using the 'Add to' feature of the selection tool, select everything that you want to keep of the structure. Invert this selection and delete everything else.
- Invert the selection back, then create a new layer.
- On this new, blank layer, keep the selection active, and create a soft gradient between dark sea-like blue and black. Then reduce the opacity of this layer.
- If you are using Picture It! then you could create a gradient effect by painting one layer black (Effects > Paint Brush > Freehand) and another layer blue, then go to Effects > Transparent Fade > Gradual to fade the black layer into the blue. Alternatively, you could simply reduce the opacity of the underwater layer by going to Effects > Transparent Fade > Even.
- As a final touch, if you have the facility, set the top layer blending mode to Multiply.

You will need:

A picture of the Parthenon or a similar ancient monument.

To complete this effect:

- Select the Parthenon shape as in the above example.
- Create a new layer.
- Set the new layer's opacity to 75% (and to Multiply if possible).
- Paint over the blocks one by one with a hard-edged brush. If you still have the shape selected then you won't be able to go over the edges.

The Statue of Liberty

Trick 13: Lady Liberty catches the Big One

You will need:

- One Statue of Liberty or other statue.
- One big fish.

To complete the effect:

1. Draw around the fish, using the lasso tool.

2. Copy and paste the fish across to the picture of the Statue of Liberty, as a new layer.

3. Resize the picture to the appropriate (or inappropriate!) scale.

4. If your edges aren't what you want them to be, select and delete the rough edges using the marquee and/or lasso tools. More precise areas should be carefully deleted with a soft-edge eraser.

5. Now we have to get the Lady Liberty to hold the fish, for which she'll have to put down her torch. First, use the rectangular marquee tool to select around the torch. We're going to copy this and make a layer to work in, so we can preserve the original hand (for now!) and concentrate on cutting out the torch.

6. Copy and paste the selection into a new layer, and turn off other layers so that you can concentrate on cutting out the torch.

7. Using a Lasso tool, cut out the torch. Note that you'll have to guess where some of the torch edges are. We'll have to build the rest of the torch where the fingers are covering. Invert the selection (Photoshop or Paint Shop Pro: CTRL+SHIFT+I, Selection > Invert in PhotoImpact), and delete the extraneous outer part of the layer.

8. Using the Clone tool, follow the lines of the torch up to cover up the fingers. To straighten lines, simply choose another clone point and reapply.

9. Continue using the clone tool to fill in the dark areas under the torch. Since most of this is in shadow, it shouldn't be that difficult to fill in. Now use a smaller clone brush to copy details from the underside of the torch to fill in where the fingers were holding the torch. Delete the blue sections of sky that show through the torch railings by selecting with the Magic Wand tool and deleting. Now we have a torch ready for Liberty to lay down at her feet so she can properly hold the fish.

10. Drag the torch to where you want Liberty to put it. In this case, we dragged it to her opposite arm, and used the Free Transform tool to turn it to the appropriate angle. With the background layer active, use the Lasso tool to cut a piece of the Lady's dress larger than the edge of the torch. Cut and paste the new layer on top of the torch, so it looks like it is actually resting on the book in her left arm.

If the new layer isn't automatically pasted on top of the torch, simply drag it to the top of the list of layers so that it covers the torch and matches up to the dress beneath.

12. Now we cut around her fingers, and copy and paste them into new layers. If you hide the background layer, you'll see the fingers that will be grabbing the fish and holding it up in the air. If you are using PhotoImpact, you will need to duplicate the base layer into a separate document, in this duplicate image make the selection around the fingers using the Lasso tool, and then paste the fingers back into your original document. Use the Clone brush to cover the existing fingers and torch with the blue sky.

13. Hide all of the layers other than the fish and the fingers, and move the fingers until they look like they might be somewhat of a natural hold. Once satisfied, we'll erase the extra parts of the hand, and add a bit of shadow with the paintbrush in the palm of the hand.

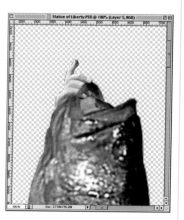

14. Now all that's left is to get rid of the parts we don't need again. To get rid of the torch, we'll use the Clone tool and use the sky as the anchor with which to paint. We don't need to be too fussy, since the fish is covering the majority of the arm. Voila!

The statue took nearly a decade to build, and was finished in 1884, in a totally different continent from the one it occupies today!

The statue is 150ft tall.

The seven spikes in the crown of the statue represent the seven seas.

Trick 14: Planet of the japes

You will need:

- An image of someone on the beach.
- An image of the Statue of Liberty.

To complete the effect:

- Cut round the upper portion of the Statue of Liberty.
- Copy and paste the statue onto the beach image. Use the move tool to drag it to an appropriate position.
- Play around with the color saturation until the statue matches its surroundings.
- Use the distort tool (Effect > Warping command in PhotoImpact) to drag sand up around the base of the statue to give the impression it is buried in the sand.
- Blur the edges and add some noise in the area around the join to better hide it.

Trick 15: Foam fingers

You will need:

- An image of the Statue of Liberty.

To complete the effect:

- Create a new layer above the background. On this layer use the shape tool to draw a series of rectangles in the vicinity of the statue's hand – one to form the palm of the glove, one to form the pointing finger, and smaller ones to form the other fingers.
- Use the move and rotate tools to position them over the statue's hand.
- Use the brush to draw in the other bits of the glove and complete its shape.
- Create a new text layer and write the text that will appear on the glove. Drag and reshape as appropriate until it is correctly positioned.
- Duplicate the palm section of the glove and place the copy behind, dragged slightly to one side, to make it look three-dimensional.
- Cut away a small section of the duplicated layer and fill the gap in using the brush tool, with black color set to about 60% opacity – this will create a small area of shadow on the statue's arm to complete the 3D effect.

Hooray for Hollywood!

Trick 16: Your name on Hollywood Boulevard

You will need:

- One photograph of Hollywood Boulevard.
- One photograph of man with hammer and chisel.

To complete this effect:

1. Open your image of Hollywood Boulevard, create a new layer and use the Clone tool to clone out original name.

2. Activate the Text tool, and type your name onto the canvas.

3. Alter the color of the text so it is the same as the outline of the star. Photoshop users can highlight the text, click on the text color icon and then select the border's color using the color picker. Paint Shop Pro users can do this too when the text dialog box appears.

4. Before going any further, we have to simplify the text layer. To do this go to Layer > Simplify Layer. We also need to alter the perspective of the text. In Paint Shop Pro, go into Effects > Geometric Effects >Perspective > Vertical and enter a value of -100. Photoshop users, select Edit >Transform > Perspective and use the corner handles to change the text.

5. Open the file with the person chiseling, use the lasso tools to select the person and copy and paste this into a new layer in the Hollywood image.

6. Using the Polygon Lasso Tool (Point To Point in Paint Shop Pro), make a selection around the man. With a soft edge eraser remove the background, leaving just the man with his hammer and chisel. Scale the man so that he fits proportionally in with the current scene, and then position his chisel over the last letter of your name.

7. Using the Levels command alter the man's appearance so it fits together with the sunny but shady day.

8. Select the Background layer and use the Burn tool to add shadows between and around the man's legs. Using a lasso tool, draw a selection around the chisel and part of the hand. Create a new layer, and fill the selection with black.

9. Move the shadow to the left slightly, and move the shadow layer beneath the hand. As a final step, use the Gaussian Blur filter to soften the shadow and adjust the Opacity of the shadow layer to around 59%.

To receive a star, an individual must be nominated by a family member, or friends, studios, managers, or agents. Each year between 12 and 25 names are chosen.

The Hollywood Walk of Fame, like so much in that incredible town, was a publicity stunt.

The stars now recognize achievements in the movies, television, recording, radio, and theater.

Each star is inlaid into a 3 foot-square black terrazzo marble square.

The Hollywood sign was built in 1923 and read Hollywoodland. It was a sales tool to sell property in the area. It worked!

Trick 17: Poppy Goes to Hollywood

You will need:

- One Hollywood (or other large) Sign.
- One troublemaking (but cute) dog.

To complete the effect:

- Select the letter you want to manipulate with the Magic Wand tool, and copy and paste it into a new layer (to make sure we don't mess up the original).
- Using the Marquee tool, cut off the part of the letter you won't be needing. We are making our "D" into an "F," so remove the part that is not F-like. Drag it off to the side rather than deleting, because we might need parts of it later.
- Using pieces of the "D", cut, move, and rotate parts that will become part of the "F". Copy the top "F" bar to make the second "F" bar.
- Using the cloning tool, use parts of the solid piece of your new "F" to erase lines. Trim the letter as necessary. Note: if necessary, hide the other layers so that the "F" is easier to differentiate as you work on it.
- Make the background layer active. Again using the clone tool—carefully—start filling in the background. Where there would be a support grid, "build" a new one by cloning bits of the existing support grid. Delete the extra parts of the "D" and further trim the letter "F" as necessary.
- Ok, now let's insert our culprit. Using the lasso (polygonal or regular) tool, cut out the puppy and paste her in the Hollywoof landscape. Resize as necessary.
- Select and delete any of the bad edges, using lasso tools and your eraser. Erase the body of the puppy where it would be behind the trees. Add appropriate touches of shadow with a brush set to Darken, 5 or 10 percent. You won't need much on a shot like this, where shadows aren't too omnipresent.
- Crop the photo to make it more dramatic. There you have it!

Trick 18: Hungry dog

You will need:

- One Hollywood (or other large) Sign.
- One troublemaking (but cute) dog.

To complete the effect:

- Insert the puppy into the image as above.
- Select the "D" as in the steps above.
- Place the "D" in the puppy's mouth. Trim where necessary, and rotate a bit to make it seem more like the puppy actually pulled it off the sign.
- Fill in the supports using the clone tool.
- Give the "D" a shadow where appropriate.

Big Ben

Trick 19: Seeing Red in London

You will need:

- A landmark such as Big Ben that looks good without too much color.

This image contains two classic London icons... one London bus and one Big Ben. Apart from being prone to turning up late and then arriving three at a time, the main thing about London buses is that they are red. Big Ben, on the other hand, is an old historic monument; you could say timeless – which is an ironic thing to be for a clock!

To complete the effect:

1. Bring up your program's Hue/Saturation adjustment window. In Photoshop, this is achieved using CTRL/⌘+U. In Paint Shop Pro, use SHIFT+H to bring up the equivalent dialog. In PhotoImpact this shortcut is CTRL/⌘+E.

Photoshop Elements

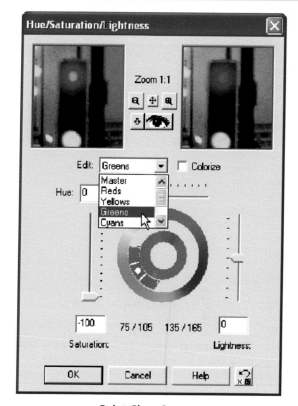

Paint Shop Pro

2. In Photoshop and Paint Shop Pro, use the drop-down menu to select different groups of colors to alter. One after another, select the Greens, Cyans, Blues and finally the Magentas channel. Each time, move the saturation slider as far down as possible and then go onto the next color.

3. In PhotoImpact you will need to select the appropriate color range, and then adjust its saturation accordingly. If you're using Picture It, you'll need to select all the red elements of the picture using the Cutout > Color Selection function, this will put all the red objects on a separate layer. With the main image selected go to Touchup > Hue and Saturation and reduce the saturation for the rest of the image.

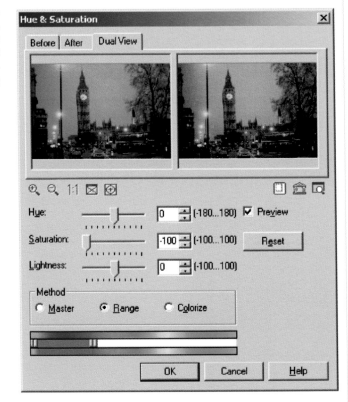

4. Finally, tweak the image to your liking. For example, you could boost the red elements in the image by increasing their saturation level. Also, if the image is a little dark, then you can simply go back to the Master selection and move the Lightness slider to the right.

Any Londoner will tell you: Big Ben is a bell, mate! It is housed in St Stephen's Tower, London.

The bell itself is the huge 13th bell which dongs the hour.

Big Ben first chimed from the tower on 31st May 1859.

The bell was named after Sir Benjamin Hall, a big-boned politician of the time.

Trick 20: The Time Warp

You will need:

- An unspoiled landmark ripe for the Dali treatment.

To complete the effect:

- Use a distorting filter or effect; such as Photoshop's Wave filter or PhotoImpact's Ripple effect to apply a light wavy pattern horizontally.
- Now select the face of the clock with an appropriate tool and copy it to a new layer.
- We'll now stretch the newly copied clock face. In Photoshop apply the Liquify tool, in PhotoImpact you can use the Effect > Warping command. And there you have it – Big Ben through the eyes of Dali.

Trick 21: Time flies

You will need:

- A subject to create a feeling of depth of field.

To complete the effect:

- Make a cutout of the subject – it doesn't need to be that precise.
- Copy and paste the cutout onto the background image, and give the layer the name Person.
- Make a duplicate of the Person layer, and merge that duplicate with the background.
- Apply a radial blur to the background (in Photoshop, that is Filters > Blur > Radial Blur).
- Having done this, select the person on their layer (in Photoshop Ctrl+clicking on the layer in the palette will automatically select the person for you).
- Expand the selection by 5 pixels (Selection) > Modify > Expand).
- Feather the selection by 15 pixels.
- Invert the selection.
- Press DELETE. This will do enough to make the person seem part of the image while also retaining enough image clarity for them to stand out.

Golden Gate Bridge

Trick 22: The ultimate birthday banners

You will need:

■ A suspension bridge of some kind

To complete the effect:

1. First open up the Bridge picture.

2. Draw a rectangular marquee the width of the distance between the two bridge stanchions and the height of the nearest one.

3. Open a new layer and turn off the visibility of the background layer. Then fill the selected area in the new layer with a strong color (I've chosen dark blue).

4. Select the text tool and write your greeting on the blue background. I suggest you choose a strong contrast color (for example this gold color). Try to make the lettering big and spread it across the square.

5. You can also add a couple of trim effects at this stage on new layers – I have put a couple of lines in. If your program (Photoshop, Photoshop Elements) requires you to simplify type layers to make them part of the main image, do so now.

6. If any remain, merge all the layers that make up the banner. Now apply a texture filter to give a fabric effect. In Photoshop this is the 'Texturizer' under the Texture submenu, in Paint Shop Pro, go to the Effects > Texture Effects > Texture… dialog and select an appropriate texture from the dialog.

We'll use these steps to create the wind ripple effect:

- Now create two new layers. Call the first Dodge and set the layer option (from the drop down box on the layer palette) to Color Dodge. Call the second Burn and set to Color Burn in the option drop-down.

- Select the airbrush tool. Set the options (top of the screen) to a soft edged brush, size 100, Normal mode and pressure of 10%.

- Select the elliptical marquee and set the feathering to 20 px (at the top of the screen).

7. With the Dodge layer selected, make an elliptical selection cutting through the top corners of the banner. Using the airbrush (with the gold color selected as the foreground color) draw along the bit of the dotted line that cuts through the banner. This should leave a light smear.

8. Invert the selection. Now select the Burn layer and draw along the dotted line in the same way. This should leave a dark smear on the other side of the line.

9. Continue making gradually bigger ellipses and dodge and burn your way down the banner in exactly the same way.

10. When you have finished, merge the visible layers and Erase any areas where you went over the edges.

11. Use a distort tool to reduce the bottom width (to give the effect of being stretched between two mountings).

12. Switch the visibility of the background layer back on.

13. With the banner layer selected, distort it so that it fits the stanchions on your bridge.

The Golden Gate Bridge is neither golden, nor a gate. It spans the Golden Gate Strait, which is approximately 1 mile wide.

80,000 miles of wire are included in the bridge's cabling.

Trick 23: Painting the Golden Gate Bridge

Trick 24: Golden Gate Flying Race

To complete the effect:

- Open the source image and duplicate the background layer.
- Take a picture of an easel (or perhaps a TV, camera viewfinder etc), cut it out and paste it onto your original background.
- Scale and position your easel (or equivalent).
- Place your copied background above the easel layer, then use the distort tool to scale it and fit it to the easel.
- Apply a paint-like filter (In Photoshop, perhaps Paint Daubs or Watercolor).
- Erase around the edge of the 'painting' to create an unfinished or artistic effect (being careful not to reveal anything that might have been on your easel before)!

To complete the effect:

- Open the background image.
- Duplicate the back layer.
- On the duplicate layer, cut around the bridge and delete the bits that are not bridge.
- Cut out the plane from another image. Copy and paste it onto the bridge image.
- Make multiple copies of the plane layer.
- Scale and position each one and with each new plane layer use the Hue/Saturation adjustment to alter the color of the plane.
- Place some in front of the cutout image (foreground) and some behind the bridge.
- You can also duplicate each plane layer and add a little motion blur to the backmost layer of each plane.

Golden Gate Bridge

Trick 25: Kayaking across Golden Gate

You will need:

- One famous bridge span.
- One courageous man in a kayak.

To complete the effect:

1. Using a Lasso tool, roughly cut out around your subject (and his dog) in their kayak.

2. Paste and resize the cutout image on the water under the bridge in a new layer.

3. Trim around the cutout with the eraser to get rid of parts of the background.

4. Make a copy of the kayak layer and flip it vertically. Change its opacity to 30 percent. This is the beginning of our reflection in the bay.

5. To make the reflection layer more water-like, apply a ripple or wave effect. In Photoshop, choose Filter > Distort > Ocean Ripple. Since the water isn't that rough, the effect applied should be mild, too. (In Photoshop Elements, use the filters palette, in Paint Shop Pro, click through Effects > Geometric Effects > Wave).

6. Using Transform, distort the reflection backwards slightly.

Here's the final image.

The total length of the bridge is 8981 ft – or 1.7 miles.

The bridge weighs 887,000 tons.

Trick 26: East/West Sunset

To complete the effect:

- Using the lasso tools and erasers, cut out the background behind the bridge.
- Paste in a new layer behind the bridge, such as the sunset shown here.
- The bridge will need some contrast and brightness adjustments, depending on what value the new background sports. In this case, we chose a dark background, so lowering the brightness of the bridge image makes it more compatible.
- Where necessary, use a Color and Darken value paintbrush to meld colors of the bridge.

Trick 27: Lighting design

To complete the effect:

- Photoshop Elements is excellent for carrying out lighting designs. Let's light up the Golden Gate Bridge as if it were New Year!
- First we're going to have to create a faux night-time effect. Something simple should do. Open the Hue/Saturation dialog and play with the settings until you have a satisfactory night-time effect. I simply set the darkness level to –40, but you might want to play with the Hue level to make your image more blue.
- Create a new layer (Layer > New) and call it Lights.
- In the Layer Styles palette, select Outer Glows from the drop-down menu, and choose the Simple Glow. You won't see any effect yet, but what this serves to do is make our brushstrokes more luminous!
- Choose a suitably shaped brush, pick a color, and dab on the lights where you want them to be! It really is up to you. You might want to choose a simple small round brush, but on my picture I chose a Star brush at 80 pixels in the foreground. As the lights receded into the distance, I shifted the size of the brush by 10 pixels, so going 80, 70, 60, 50 and so on into the background.
- I used a very pale yellow initially, and then moved on to a more orangey color for the streetlights.

Venice

Trick 28: Dry Venice

You will need:

- A photo of a canal, preferably Venice.
- A photo of any back street.

To complete the effect:

1. Open both the canal scene and your street scene and copy the street as a layer above the Venice scene. Resize your street scene if necessary so that it covers the Venice image.

2. Make the "road" layer semi-transparent so we can see what we're doing.

3. Then select the transform or distort command and pull the corner points so that the road fits the shape of the canal. If you do not have a distort command then you could try rotating the road image until it fits the shape of the canal.

4. If you've got them, then this is another excellent opportunity to use masks. In PhotoImpact you do this by selecting the street layer, then click CTRL/⌘+ K to choose Mask mode, and then use black paint to cover the areas that you want to be hidden, when you come out of Mask mode, these elements will have magically disappeared. If you do not have a masking facility then carefully erase the road where the buildings should be on top. Use the undo facility if you go wrong, but don't worry too much about the car and boat areas.

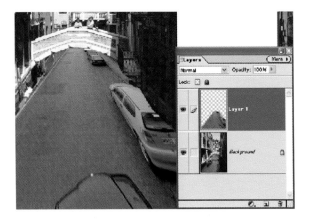

5. Switch the opacity of the base layer up to 100% and make any final changes to your edges.

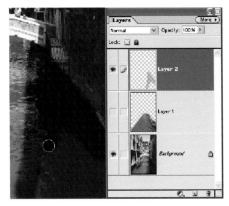

6. Turn the road layer's visibility off and with a soft brush, fill in the areas where there are shadows on the canal. If you can, do it in black, then reduce the opacity of the layer afterwards.

7. Using the clone tool, remove the especially squished cars in the foreground of the shot, and the boat on the other.

8. Use the Burn tool to darken any areas you're not too happy with – we'll call it shadow!

Venice is built on 117 small islands

It has 150 canals and 409 bridges.

Venice is actually very small, covering only 3 square miles.

Trick 29: New York Canal

You will need:

- One photo of Venice
- One Statue of Liberty

To complete the effect:

- Create a new layer from the background.
- Select the whole of the area bounded by the bridge and the buildings to the left and right – due to its shape, the magnetic lasso is especially suitable.
- Cut away all this area.
- Copy the image of the Statue of Liberty onto a new layer – place this layer behind the Venice layer and use the move tool to position it so that the statue is nicely in the center of the hole in the top layer.
- As the waters of Venice and New York are of different colors, use the clone stamp tool to copy the shade of the Venice waters and paint over the New York waters with about 70% opacity.

Trick 30: Pulling the plug on Venice

You will need:

- One photo of Venice
- A picture of a bath plug

To complete the effect:

- Use the selection tools to cut out the plug and chain.
- Copy and paste the plug onto the picture of Venice – you might have to do some very intricate erasing with the eraser tool to wipe out every trace of the background from the plug picture.
- Use the elliptical marquee selection tool to select an oval-shaped area below where the plug is hanging.
- Apply a swirl filter to this area. (Effect > 2D > Whirlpool in PhotoImpact).
- Blur the edges of the selected area.
- Darken the center with the Burn tool or equivalent.

The Colosseum

Trick 31: When in Rome...

You will need:

- One historical Roman ruin.
- One lounging friend.

To complete the effect:

1. Using the polygonal lasso tool, cut out around your lounging friend.

2. Paste and resize your friend on top of the Roman ruin in a new layer.

3. Trim around your friend with the lasso tool and eraser to get rid of parts of the background.

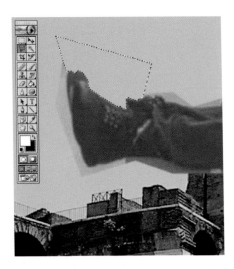

4. It takes a lot of work to keep one's head up, so we'll be helpful and draw a pillow for your friend. Or better yet, take a picture of a pillow, and cut and paste it into a new layer in the image.

5. Move this layer under your friend's layer, and using transform tools such as Rotate, Perspective and Distort, manipulate the pillow to be in the same direction and perspective as the person sleeping. Trim the excess pillow on the opposite side of his head.

6. Once your parts are in place, use a dark paintbrush at low Opacity (or better yet, the Burn tool) to put shadows on the building, our sleeper, and the pillow. And now he's peacefully sleeping on the comfy ruin.

The Colosseum was big enough to seat 50,000 people. It did indeed host fights to the death between prisoners and wild beasts.

The area of the building is an ellipse 790 feet in circumference.

Construction on the Colosseum began in the year 72 AD and was completed eight years later.

There are four storeys, each with different architecture. The first storey is Doric, the second Ionic, the third Corinthian, the fourth is a mix.

Trick 32: Yankee Stadium

You will need:

- One historical monument that you wish to drag into the 21st Century

To complete the effect:

- Select the type tool, and choose a solid looking font, in a suitably large font size.
- To choose a color for the lettering, select a stone shade from the ruins themselves.
- Type whatever text you like and position the characters to follow the arc of the stadium: In PhotoImpact you need to choose the Horizontal Deform mode, and then drag the corner handles until your text is sitting convincingly over your monument. In some programs you may need to make each letter individually editable.
- Apply a suitable texture to the text, Craquelure is a good choice.
- To create a 3D effect, duplicate the text layer and place a copy of the layer behind and to the side.
- Erase the bottom of the letters that would be hidden by the brickwork.
- For extra realism use the Hue/Saturation dialog to reduce the brightness of the backmost text layer.

Trick 33: Roman dog bed

You will need:

- One picture of the Coliseum
- One cheeky pet

To complete the effect:

- Select the sky, and some of the front windows of the stadium, and copy them to a new layer above the building.
- After cutting out your subject (in this case, Oscar the dog) from its original image, paste it into inside the stadium by tucking it between the other two layers.
- Make a copy of his ear (and any other areas to overhang the walls), and paste them it in a new top layer.
- Create shadows as appropriate using the paintbrush or Burn tool. These should be both under the chin and in the windows.

L'arc de Triomphe

Trick 34: The big push

You will need:

- A picture of a friend or family member leaning or pushing against a wall.
- An impressive monument for your friend to try to push over.

To complete the effect:

1. Use the lasso tool to cut round the person's outline. If you have the option, then use a magnetic lasso to select such a tricky shape.

2. Copy and paste your subject onto a new layer in your monument image and paste your subject, position them as though they were leaning against a wall.

3. Duplicate the monument layer, and on this new layer use the polygonal lasso tool to select an area to be pushed.

4. We'll cut this section out, and then paste it back into our image, but this time on its own layer, so click through Edit > Cut, then Edit > Paste. Get rid of the duplicated monument layer.

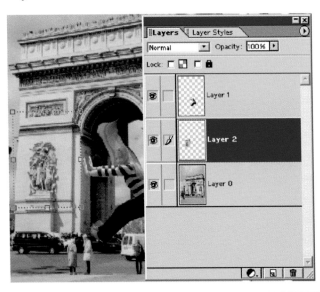

5. Rotate the selection slightly to look askew, and in Photoshop apply a drop shadow to this layer. In other programs you can use a soft, dark brush at low opacity to carefully paint in some shadows.

6. Finally, make a new layer above your skewed layer. Use the lasso tool to select areas where you want additional cracks to be added. Fill the selection with a darker shade of the wall colour and, in Photoshop, apply an inner shadow to the layer.

The construction of the Arc de Triomphe in Paris was ordered in 1806 by Napoleon, the French emperor.

The construction was completed in 1836, after a lengthy pause from 1814 to 1826.

On November 11th 1920, the body of an unknown soldier was buried under the Arc de Triomphe.

The Flame of Remembrance on the tomb of the unknown soldier is rekindled every day at 6pm by war veterans and soldiers.

Trick 35: Le Night Club

You will need:

- One national monument that's ready for a trendy makeover.

To complete the effect:

- In the Brightness/Contrast dialog set the brightness to about –50.
- Select the text tool and use a suitably glamorous font to insert the name of your club. In PhotoImpact, you'll find some great neon text effects in the Easy palette Type gallery.
- Use the transform tools to skew the text so that it sits in perspective with the monument. In Picture It! you don't have the option to skew, you could type the words in groups of different size fonts to give the same sense of perspective. Then use Edit > Group and rotate the text into position.
- Select the text layer and add a Drop Shadow, Outer Glow and Bevel and Emboss (play around with the settings of each till you're happy with the effect).
- Finally, we need to render the club lights. Select the monument layer and in Photoshop go to Filter > Render > Lens Flare, Paint Shop Pro has a lens flare effect under Effects > Illumination Effects > Sunburst, and in PhotoImpact, you'll find the lens flare effect by going to Effect > Creative > Lighting. Drag the cross hairs to where you want your lens flare to appear and click OK when done. Repeat this process to achieve multiple lens flares adjusting the brightness as desired.

Trick 36: Safari Holiday

You will need:

- One national monument image.
- One picture of animals.

To complete the effect:

- We'll start by making a selection around our animals. In Photoshop 7 you could use the Extract tool to do this, by going to Filter > Extract. In all other programs, I'm afraid you'll need to take the slightly more laborious route of using a lasso to select the animals.
- Copy and paste the animals into your monument image. Use the Transform tools to adjust the scale so that the animals fit in with their surroundings. If you wanted, you could make them slightly larger than life for comic effect.
- Now you need to add some shadows beneath the animals. The best way to do this is with the Burn tool, or you could use a soft dark brush, set to low opacity to subtly paint the shadows in.
- The thought bubbles are made out of solid white ellipses. In Photoshop use the Ellipse tool to make them, in Picture It! you need to go to Insert > Shape, while in PhotoImpact you'd use the Path Drawing tool.
- It's time to add the witty caption to amuse friends and family. Simply type this straight over the largest ellipse and wait for the sound of laughter.

The Great Wall of China

Trick 37: Dropping in for a stroll

You will need:

- One stunning landscape, such as the Great Wall of China.
- One photo of a hand.
- A picture of someone in a "being dropped in" position.

To complete the effect:

1. Open the picture of your landscape, and create a new layer. This picture of the Great Wall of China has some people in the foreground that we need to remove, so we'll do this using the Clone tool.

The Clone tool may differ slightly in different programs, but the principle is always the same: you need to select an area of your image to be the source of the clone and then paint over the area that you wish to cover. The source of the clone is set in the following ways: ALT-click in Photoshop, RIGHT/CTRL-click in Paint Shop Pro, and SHIFT-click when using PhotoImpact. Unfortunately, Picture It! does not have a Clone tool.

2. Open your picture of a person. To get a photo of someone in this position, you'll probably need to take the shot especially, unless your friends are prone to standing around like this. Once you have the picture, you need to make a selection around the figure. Use the lasso tool to do this, then invert the selection so his background area is selected and hit DELETE. In Picture It! you would do this by clicking Select opposite area.

3. Copy and paste your figure into your landscape image. Resize the man so he is just a little bigger than everyone else and position him over the people that you cloned out.

4. Open your hand image, and again use the lasso to cut around the hand. If your background is a consistently colored area, then you could use the Magic Wand tool. Click anywhere on the background of the hand and all areas within the same color range will be highlighted, to adjust the selection, click the Add to or Subtract from selection buttons. When you are happy, invert the selection and copy the hand.

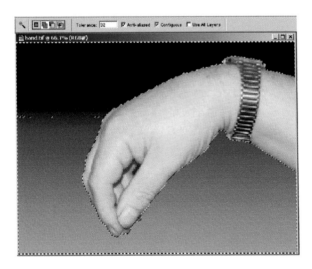

5. Paste the hand into your main image; position the fingers just above the man's shoulder. Move the hand layer beneath the layer with your person on it.

6. We now need to add some shading to make the picture look more realistic. Use a soft dark brush at low opacity to create shadow behind the man's head and on the ground below his feet. When doing this, it's best to create a separate layer for your shadows. Place the shadow over the man's face, blur the paint slightly, and then move this layer so that the shadow is behind the man's head. Finally, use the move tool to nudge the blurred shadow up about 10 or so pixels.

7. Here's one final trick, which works in Photoshop 7 and Paint Shop Pro only, you can use this on the hand and person layers to tidy up the pasted images. In Photoshop, you'll find this option under Layer > Matting > Defringe, in Paint Shop Pro go to Selections > Matting > Defringe, and then enter a value of 2.

Get this: the first section of the Great Wall took ten years to build, and its construction proceeded at the rate of about one mile per day.

The Great Wall is 4,500 miles long.

One section of the Wall climbs mountain ridges at an angle of 70 degrees.

The Great Wall is on average 15 to 30 feet high, and 15 to 25 feet wide.

Trick 38: Carpeting the Great Wall

To complete the effect:

- Create a carpet design; mine is randomly colored flowers. Click through Edit > Define Pattern in Photoshop, in Paint Shop Pro open the Pattern dialog by clicking the Styles button in the Color palette, and you'll see your pattern there.
- Make a new layer in your monument image and make a rough lasso selection along the first plane onto which you wish to lay your carpet. For example in the Great Wall of China image, this selection would be from the foreground of the picture down to the first bend to the right.
- Go to Edit > Fill and choose your pattern to fill the shape. Adjust the perspective of the carpet using the Transform tools, so that the carpet sits along the surface.
- Create a new layer and another rough selection for the other planes on your monument. Again, fill with your carpet pattern, but scale it right down to create perspective.
- Make the carpet layer invisible and use the magic wand tool to select the ground. Use the zoom tool to help you make your selections and set the wand's tolerance level low. Keep the Add to selection button pushed in.
- Once you're happy with your selection, go back to the carpet layer, invert the selection and hit DELETE in order to get rid of the carpet offcuts.
- To include the existing shadows, change the layer blending mode to Multiply.

Trick 39: Great Wall of Venice

To complete the effect:

- This one's similar to the carpet. As above, select your area of water, and paste several copies of it on to your monument, and shape it up with the transform tools. You won't have to worry about perspective!
- Keep the layer blending mode as Normal and, as before, use the magic wand tool or the lasso tool to select every part of the monument you want under water. As before, invert the selection, and press DELETE.
- Create splashes around peoples' feet and ankles, using a small white brush at around 50% opacity.

Hoover Dam

Trick 40: Bath-time at the Hoover Dam

You will need:

- One national monument
- One bouncing baby

To complete the effect:

1. Draw around the baby, using the freehand selection tool.

2. Copy and paste the baby across to the picture of the monument, as a new layer.

3. Resize the picture to the appropriate (or inappropriate!) scale.

4. Select and delete any of the really horrible edges, using the marquee and lasso tools, depending on whether you want a straight edge.

5. Carefully delete the more delicate areas with a soft eraser.

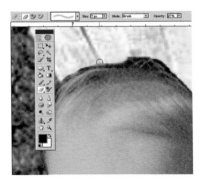

6. Flip the layer vertically and drag it to match the bottom of the existing layer. This will be our reflection!

7. Reduce the opacity to 30%.

8. Apply a ripple or wave effect to the reflection. If you're using Photoshop Elements, you'll find this under Filter > Ocean Ripple, in Paint Shop Pro use Effects > Geometric Effects > Wave, and in PhotoImpact you can use Effect > 2D > Ripple.

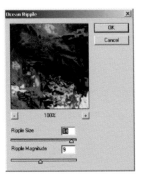
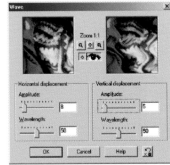

9. As a Photoshop Elements detail, muss the bottom a little using the Smudge tool.

10. Finally add a little white paint for froth, as desired! Remember to keep the opacity low.

There is 45,000 lbs of pressure per square foot at the base of the dam.

The Hoover Dam is 726 feet from top to bottom.

The towers are 40 feet high, making the total height 766 feet.

The Dam weighs over 6.5 million tons.

It took five years to complete the dam, which was completed in March 1936.

Trick 41: Attack of the Giant Babies!

To complete the effect:

- Drag the baby to the top of the dam.
- Select the areas of the dam the baby would be behind. Delete them.
- Copy the Baby Layer. Drag it below the normal layer in the Layer Palette.
- Set its brightness to 0. Apply a Gaussian Blur.
- Delete the areas you don't want in shadow.

Trick 42: The Writing on the Wall

To complete the effect:

- Create a graffiti design, and drag it onto your Hoover Dam picture.
- Click through Filter > Distort > Spherize and set the palette to around –30. In Paint Shop Pro a quick Pinch would do the trick, at a pinch! This is Effect > 3D > Pinch in PhotoImpact
- Set the Layer Blending Mode to Multiply.
- Select and delete areas that should be behind rock.
- As with the first baby reflection, duplicate the layer and flip it vertically. Set the opacity to 30%
- Apply a Glass filter or effect and choose a distortion that sits well on the water. Frosted is a good bet. In Paint Shop Pro, click through Effects > Geometric Effects > Wave once again.

United States Capitol

Trick 43: Congress cake

You will need:

- A picture of the US Capitol, or any building with a dome-shaped roof.

To complete the effect:

1. Open the congress picture and make a copy of the background layer – call it building. If you have guides, as in Photoshop and Paint Shop Pro, drag a guide from the ruled border at the left-hand side. Drag it over the middle of the picture, so that runs through the center of the tip of the dome.

2. Using the lasso tool, follow the lines of the dome and select a quadrant section. Then press DELETE.

3. Create a new layer and call it sponge. Make sure the layer is below the building layer. Draw a rectangular marquee from the guideline outwards, covering the right-hand side of the 'hole'.

4. Now to create a tasty-looking sponge. In Photoshop, select a foreground color of light brown and a background color of dark brown. Choose Filter > Render > Clouds. If you don't have a cloud filter don't worry too much, we'll be adding some more texture in the next step. For now, simply add some noise, which you'll find under the Filter or Effect menu. Then follow the same procedure to fill in the left-hand side of the guideline.

5. If you're using Photoshop, now go to Filter > Artistic > Underpainting and add a sandstone texture. In Paint Shop Pro you'll find that the Gravel texture works well (Effects > Texture Effects)– although its name doesn't make the cake seem very appetizing!

6. Open up a new layer and call it 'shade'. Make sure this layer is in front of the sponge layer, but behind the building layer. As before, make a rectangular selection to the right of the guide. In this selection, draw a straight horizontal graduation from black to transparent. Do the same on the left. When you have done this, set the opacity of the layer to 50%

7. Make a new layer and call it cream. Make sure this layer is behind the shade layer and in front of the sponge layer. Select a cream color and with the paintbrush draw a cream section onto the sponge. Highlight the cream with some white splodges (you can use the color dodge setting to do this).

8. To make the swirls in the cream, you could use the Liquify filter in Photoshop, the Twirl effect in Paint Shop Pro or the Warping effect in PhotoImpact.

9. Make another new layer and call it jam. Follow the same procedure only select a dark red color, drawing the jam above the cream. Use color dodge to make some lighter splodges. (As an extra touch in Photoshop, you can use the Plastic Wrap filter to make the jam look extra realistic.) Select the jam and then place a marquee around it and use the same warping tools as you just used to make the jam drip.

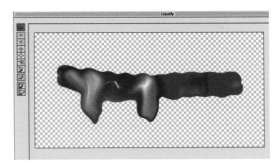

As a final touch, use the original red color with a soft airbrush to take a little of the shine out of the jam. And there you have it – a national monument that's good enough to eat!

The structure of the building evolved over a period of more than 150 years.

Before the building's construction, the site was occupied by Jenkins Hill – described by a contemporary as "a pedestal waiting for a monument."

The first low-lying Capitol building was torched by the British in 1814, after which it was rebuilt.

The final additions to the building – including the cast-iron dome – were made in 1865.

Trick 44: Stars and Lights

Trick 45: American Dream

You will need:

- One picture of the US Capitol.
- A picture of a flag or emblem.

To complete the effect:

- Cut off the top of the dome. Delete the rest of the image. Also turn off the visibility of the background image.
- On a new layer, draw an ellipse to give the dome a 3D appearance. Fill the ellipse with a faint gradient.
- On another new layer, use the eyedropper to select a color from the dome and use this to fill the background.
- In the flag picture, use the magic wand to select a white piece of the flag. Then invert the selection and copy and paste this into the picture of Congress.
- Create yet another layer, just above the flag.
- Select the polygonal lasso tool with a feather level of 50.
- Draw a triangle with the top point in the middle of the dome, running down to rest across the foot of the image. Invert the selection and fill with 50% black.
- Invert the selection back again, and then create one last layer just above the black layer. Fill this layer with white, and then reduce its opacity of this layer until the light seems to be emanating from the dome of Congress to illuminate the Stars and Stripes.

You will need:

- One inspirational national monument.
- A picture of people looking upwards.

To complete the effect:

- Open the picture of the couple.
- Cut around them and the foot of the image and drop them into the image of Congress.
- Resize and position the couple.
- Select the background image and add a Gaussian blur.
- Adjust the blur setting to a radius of 15.
- Flatten the image.

Bavarian Castle

Trick 46: Castle in the sky

You will need:

- An image of a fairytale castle, like this one in Bavaria.
- A picture of some clouds, we've used the sky from this shot of Pompeii.

To complete the effect:

Getting this right is a bit like a military exercise in camouflage. You may not be trying to hide the object, but you are attempting to make two separate elements appear to be part of the same landscape. And, like a military camouflage exercise, the same basic visual principles apply: Silhouette, Shadow, Shade, Shine, Spacing, and Size.

1. The first step is to draw a simple rectangular selection around the majority of the sky in the Pompeii picture.

2. Having done that, copy the selection and paste it over the castle.

3. Clouds tend to live up in the air, above eye level, but in our case we want ours to be below eye level, in place of the ground. To do this, flip the layer on the vertical. (Edit > Rotate and Flip > Flip Vertical in PhotoImpact).

4. We need to stretch the clouds a little to help with the illusion. Use your program's perspective adjustment to do this (Image > Transform > Perspective in Photoshop Elements).

5. Now scale up the whole of the cloud layer.

6. The problem you have now, going back to the camouflage rules, is one of shade – it's the wrong color for the scenery around it. Use a Hue/Saturation adjustment to make the images match better.

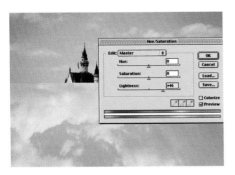

7. Now we need to deal with that silhouette. Using the eraser tool with a big, soft brush, gently remove some of the cloud. This effect is a bit like having a spray can of transparency that you apply to the cloud. Start at the top and in small movements erase the hard edge. Work your way onto the castle and gently reveal its shape leaving wisps of cloud if you want. If you make a mistake you can always undo and try again.

This was the castle that Walt Disney copied to create the Disneyland Fairytale Castle.

The foundation stone for the castle was laid on September 5, 1869 at the behest of King Ludwig II of Bayern.

The castle was never completed.

It was thought at the time that Ludwig II wasted the state's money and taxes for the building of his castles. However, it is now known the King only used money from his own personal fortune.

Trick 47: King of the Castle

You will need:

- A striking castle image.
- A subject ready to be transported to a mountain setting.

To complete the effect:

- Use the lasso tool with a feathering of 2 pixels, to cut around your subject and the rock.
- Copy and paste this selection onto your Bavarian background.
- The sun on the picture of the person is lighting up his right sleeve, while the sun on the castle is shining on the left turret, so flip your subject horizontally. Both images are now adhering to the same laws of physics.
- Move the person and the rock down and to the left so that the edges of the cut out disappear off the frame of the image.
- Select the eraser tool and run it over any bits that don't look like they should be there. Do this by magnifying sections a bit at a time.

Trick 48: Blue Moon

You will need:

- A spooky atmospheric castle.
- A mysterious femme fatale.

To complete the effect:

- In the Bavaria image, delete the original sky. Now, create a new layer and add a gradient that goes from dark blue at the top of the screen to mid blue at the bottom.
- Reduce the Saturation and Lightness of the layer until it looks like a moonlit scene.
- Select around your person, and then copy and paste her into the scene. Resize her to fit the scene. You now need to adjust her lighting so that she appears to be lit by moonlight. Use the Curves or Levels command and also reduce the Saturation and Lightness.
- Move the castle layer to the left so that the composition of the picture is balanced (the cutout of the girl will conceal the gap it leaves on the right).
- Use the shape tools to draw a white circle the size of a moon on a new layer.
- Duplicate the layer (in Photoshop, that's CTRL/⌘+J together) and apply a Gaussian Blur to one of the layers - this will give your moon an eerie glow.
- Finally, select white as a foreground color and on the same layer select the paintbrush. With soft-edged brushes of varying sizes, scatter a few stars around.

Edinburgh Castle

Trick 49: Fireworks over Edinburgh

You will need:

- One picture of Edinburgh castle.
- A picture of some jolly sparklers.

To complete the effect:

1. Make a cutout of the castle and place it on another layer, in place over the background. Select the background layer. If your program includes a Curves command (Color > Adjust > Curves in Paint Shop Pro), then open this now and drag the line towards the bottom right to darken the sky. You can achieve the same effect with the Levels command (set the input value to 194 and the output to roughly 72), or go to Format > Tone Map in PhotoImpact.

2. Copy and paste the image of the sparklers into the castle picture. Adjust the size so that the whole width fits onto the width of the castle picture. Make sure the sparklers layer is above the background and below the cutout.

3. Here is a trick if you're using Photoshop 7. Double-click on the Sparkler layer. You will see the Layer Style controls appear. Find the two sliders at the bottom. Move the upper one a little to the right. This makes the darkest pixels transparent. As you slide the slider towards the right, it makes more and more pixels transparent. By doing this, we can knock the dark background out and keep the sparklers, which in this context now look like fireworks.

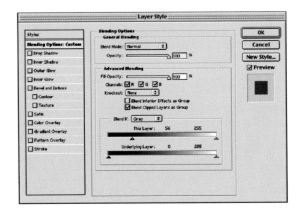

4. In all other programs, erase any parts of the image that don't look like fireworks – in our example, that includes the sundae glass. Then set the blending mode to Lighten so that the black background dissolves into our darkened sky.

5. We can still see a little too much foreground for it to be night. Create another layer on top of all the others. Use the rectangular marquee to select an area from the bottom to about halfway up. Select black as the foreground color and make a foreground to transparent gradient.

6. Alter the opacity of the gradient layer if it seems a little dark. Here is the final effect.

The site of Edinburgh Castle has shown evidence of settlements from the early bronze age.

The castle has become an icon of Scottish rule, with the English and Scots conducting their troublesome history around and about its control.

Early Edinburgh was a small village on the eastern side of the fortification, huddled close to the wall for protection.

The last action the castle saw was during the Jacobite rising in 1745, when Bonnie Prince Charlie made a doomed attempt to take the castle during his ill-fated attempt to regain the Scottish throne and defeat the English.

Trick 50: Scotland the brave

You will need:

- A photo of Edinburgh castle.

To complete the effect:

- Cut out the outline of the castle and paste it in place on another layer.
- Create a new layer and fill with navy blue. Draw a line with the polygonal lasso from one corner to the other and around the corner so that it joins up. Fill with white to make one section of the cross. Repeat the procedure with the other corners to complete the cross. In PhotoImpact you would do this by creating a navy blue rectangle to fill the whole screen and then using a white paintbrush to create the stripes.
- Use a distort filter to create a wave effect on the flag. In Photoshop, Filter > Distort > Wave is a good choice.
- Now add some highlights and shading to the flag. Use the airbrush and if you have them, the dodge and burn settings.
- When you have finished, drag the flag layer to below the castle cutout layer. Move the cutout down the screen so that the center of the cross frames the top of the castle.

Trick 51: Scottish rain

You will need:

- A cloud picture.
- A monument in a suitably rainy location.

To complete the effect:

- Paste the clouds onto the image of the castle. Move the clouds around until a nice dark bit is visible. Enhance the clouds using the Hue/Saturation or the Curves command.
- Use the eraser with an airbrush setting to rub out the bits of the cloud that obscure the castle and the skyline.
- Create a new layer in front of all the others. Fill the layer with white, add some noise, preferably a Gaussian noise, and crank up the value quite high.
- Then add a motion blur. Select a slight angle and enough blur to give all the noise a sort of brushed metal look.
- Go to the layer mode and select hard light.
- Finally reduce the saturation slightly to give it that gray Edinburgh-in-the-rain look.

Mount Rushmore

Trick 52: Pop Art Rushmore

You will need:

- One picture of Mount Rushmore, or suitable substitute.

To complete this effect:

1. Duplicate the background layer and on the new layer, go to Image > Adjustments > Threshold in Photoshop, or Colors > Adjust > Threshold in Paint Shop Pro. Use the default setting of 128.

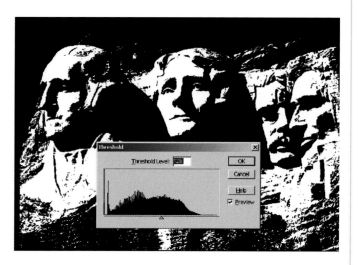

2. Set the blending mode of this layer to Multiply. This enables all the blacks to show through, and all the whites to blend in.

3. Create a new layer and call it 'Paint'. Drag it between the two layers you already have. On this layer we'll have some fun coloring in with the paintbrush. If you want to follow the Pop Art style, you have to work with flat colors – one pink for the face, one yellow for the hair, one blue for the eyes, and so on. Your paint layer will end up looking something like this:

4. A creditable accidental doodle! All the layers together look like the image opposite.

Sculptor Gutzon Borglum began work on the 5,725 foot mountain in 1927. He was 60 years old!

The monument took 14 years to create, and cost $1 million.

Over the decade and a half, Mount Rushmore underwent a weight-loss program of 800 million pounds!

The president's noses are 20 feet long, each mouth 18 feet wide and the eyes are 11 feet across.

Trick 53: Rocking out with George, Tom, Theo and Abe

You will need:

- A picture of Mount Rushmore.
- A passport picture of yourself or another presidential candidate.
- A picture of sand

To complete the effect:

- I started by adding an air of presidential gravitas in the form of a wobbly mouth, which I created using the Liquify command in Photoshop. However, this is an optional step.
- Now it's time to get into rock. Draw a rectangular marquee around the face area.
- Invert the selection and then hit DELETE. Then invert the selection back again so that you have the face selected once again. Open up the Hue/Saturation dialog and lower the Saturation right down, making the picture black and white.
- Create a new layer and then copy and paste your sand image into your selection. (Edit > Paste into in Photoshop, Edit > Paste > Into Selection in Paint Shop Pro and PhotoImpact). This will obscure your face with the sand. Set the new layer to Overlay in the layer palette options. Using the move tool, slide the sand image around until you have some consistent texture across the face.
- Now merge the two layers, (Layer > Merge Visible in Photoshop and Object > Merge All in PhotoImpact). Crop the image to remove the white edges, then copy and paste it into the Mount Rushmore picture, and finally scale your face to fit.
- Use the Eraser tool with a soft-edged airbrush of 100px and a pressure of about 50% or less. Then rub out the edges of the picture, working inwards as you go. You can choose to rub out bits of the cheek area as well to bring through the original rock.
- When you have finished 'blending' your face into the mountain, open the Hue/Saturation dialog and adjust the layer's coloring until it better matches the mountain. Finally add some extra shadows using the Burn tool and prepare to rock out with the presidents.

Trick 54: Man in the Mountain

You will need:

- One picture of a famous mountainside.
- Some images of doors and windows.

To complete the effect:

- This uses the same principles of the last exercise, except it is much simpler.
- Copy and paste the doors and windows images onto the Mount Rushmore picture.
- Lower the opacity of the windows and doors slightly so you can find good positions for them, and scale them accordingly.
- Use the eraser tool with an airbrush setting, a soft-edged brush selected and the pressure reduced. Then rub out the edges and blend them into the picture. It is useful to use the contours and shadows of the original image to nestle the new images into.

St Louis' Gateway Arch

Trick 55: Big Cat

You will need:

- A picture of an arch of some description, in this case St Louis' Gateway Arch.
- A picture of a pet

To complete the effect:

1. Select the animal using a freehand or Lasso tool.

2.

3. Scale the picture to an appropriately inappropriate size.

4. Remove unwanted areas around the main subject with the Eraser tool.

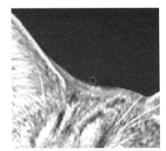

5. Draw a selection around the edges of the arch while the cat layer is still active – hit DELETE key to remove those parts of the cat (or animal) that would be hidden.

6. Repeat the above process above for the right-hand side of the arch

7. Clone out unwanted leaves from the tree while the selection is still active.

8. Add shadows on the cat to the left and right of the arch – use a polygonal selection tool to draw them, then fill them with black and soften them with a blur.

9. Adjust the brightness of the cat, using levels if possible. Darken the cat so that it blends in with the arch.

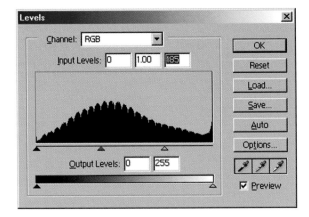

10. Draw a selection around the cat's head and move the selection (only the selection, not the contents of the selection) onto the left hand side of the arch.

11. Fill the area with black on a new layer. Blur heavily and adjust opacity to approx 60%. Remove any unwanted shadow on the cat using the eraser.

The width and height of the Gateway Arch is 630 feet.

The arch has been recorded as moving 18" in winds of 150mph.

The arch contains 886 tons of steel and 38,000 tons of concrete.

Trick 56: Red Eyes

To complete the effect:

- Flatten all the layers together.
- Create a new layer and make a selection of the cat's eyes.
- Fill the selection with red.
- Change the blending mode to Multiply, and perhaps reduce the opacity.
- Switch back to the bottom layer and remove all color by using a desaturate command.

Trick 57: Sci-fi portal

To complete the effect:

- Draw a selection around the cat, making sure you get as close to him as possible.
- Invert the selection.
- Apply a Twirl filter from an effects menu. In Photoshop, for example, Effect >Distort > Twirl, or Paint Shop Pro users go into Effect >Geometric Effects >Twirl.
- For that portal effect, apply a glass effect too. Now it looks like our monster cat is coming through some sort of 6th dimension!

The White House

Trick 58: Scottish President?

You will need:

- One picture of a stately home or other flat-based monument.
- One picture of tartan.

To complete this effect:

1. Copy your sample of tartan over to the chosen monument, placing it on a new layer.

2. Duplicate the layer and place it next to the original.

3. Flatten those layers so that there is only one tartan layer.

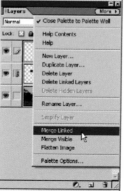

4. Repeat steps 2 and 3 until you have completely covered your monument (don't worry about the surrounding sky etc.).

5. Bring out the circular effect of the façade by selecting a rectangle over it...

(Here we've made the tartan temporarily transparent to help locate the right area of the White House)

6. ...then applying a cylindrical effect to that selection. In Photoshop, this is achieved with the Filter > Render > 3D Transform and the cylinder button.

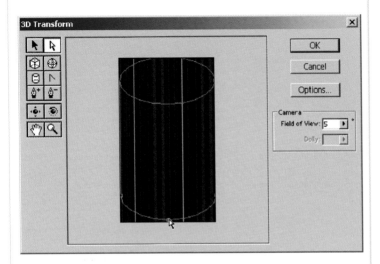

7. In Paint Shop Pro, a similar effect can be achieved with the Effect > Geometric Effects > Cylinder - Vertical option.

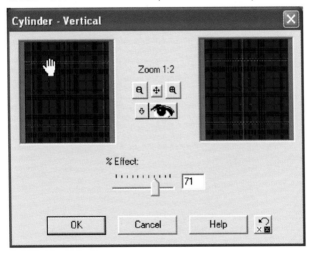

8. Make the tartan layer invisible for a while. Working on the monument's own layer, select the entire area of the monument you would like to "entarten", then invert the selection.

9. Return to the tartan layer, make it visible, and press delete.

10. Set the layer blending mode to Multiply.

11. There we have our Tartan House!

There are 132 rooms, 35 bathrooms, and 6 levels in the residence. There are also 412 doors, 147 windows, 28 fireplaces, 8 staircases, and 3 elevators.

President Theodore Roosevelt officially gave the White House its current name in 1901.

The White House requires 570 gallons of paint to cover its outside surface.

Trick 59: Total eclipse

Trick 60: Haunted garden

To complete this effect:

- Create a new layer from the background.
- Reduce the brightness level of this layer to make the scene look dark.
- Use the shape tool to draw a circle in the sky, with a white fill.
- Draw a similar but ever so slightly smaller circle, with a black fill. Position it on top of the white circle – try and get them as concentric as you can. (In Photoshop, you can achieve a perfect concentric effect by using the circular Selection tool and the Select > Modify > Contract option.)
- Select the white circle and add a Gaussian blur filter to create the "corona" effect.

To complete this effect:

- Create a new layer from the background and darken it as above.
- As the light levels during an eclipse and during the night differ, use the magic wand tool to select the sky and fill the selection with 85% opacity black. There are a lot of fiddly little areas of sky peeking between tree branches – unless you have a very steady hand and an incredible level of patience it might be easier just to paint over these with 100% opacity black.
- Use a small brush to paint on the stars. Use varying levels of brightness (80% down to about 40%), to give a perception of depth to the night sky.
- Open up a picture of a girl (or headless horseman), and use the lasso to select the figure and copy it onto a new layer on the White House picture.
- Increase the brightness of this layer, and add a slight Gaussian blur to make her look "ethereal".

Eiffel Tower

Trick 61: Room with a view

Here's how to convince people that you went to Paris and had the best view of it from your window.

You will need:

- A good picture of the Eiffel Tower.
- A suitably picturesque window.

To complete the effect:

1. We need to start by selecting the area in the window image into which we'll paste the tower. Make a selection around the view, in our case we'll leave the roof in the foreground to give a little more perspective.

2. Open the Eiffel Tower picture; go to Select > All and then Edit > Copy. Return to the window image, and go to Edit > Paste Into.

3. Scale the tower to fit the window using the Free Transform tool, and then position it in the center of the window.

4. For an authentic touch, let's add a reflection in the window panes. Use the polygonal lasso to make a selection around the glass in the top pane of the left window and having done so, keep the SHIFT button depressed while also selecting the glass in the middle pane on the left window.

5. With your pane selection still active, create a new layer and then click Edit > Paste Into and then scale the tower into place. To make a reflected image, click Edit > Transform > Flip Horizontal. Press OK.

6. We need to distort the reflection a little, and make it slightly see-through. Use the lasso tool to draw around the windowpane again and then use a Ripple or Wave filter to add some slight distortion to the edges. Then reduce the opacity of the layer to about 60%.

Repeat the same procedure for the two top panes on the right window and voila – a perfect view of the Eiffel Tower!

The Eiffel Tower took two years to build, and was finished in 1889 for the Universal Exhibition.

The Tower is made up of 18,038 steel pieces, held together with 2.5 million rivets!

From top to toe the Tower is 986 feet tall, plus 6 inches, depending on the heat!

The Tower weighs 7,000 tons – and 1,000 tons were removed during the centennial restoration.

A repaint job takes place every 7 years, with 50 tons of paint.

Trick 62: Parisian bunting

To complete the effect:
- Create a new layer in the Eiffel Tower picture.
- You now need to draw a wavy line to be the base of your ribbon. In Photoshop you could use the Pen tool, and in Paint Shop Pro use the Draw tool with Freehand Line selected in the Tool Options window. In PhotoImpact, use the Path Drawing tool with the Selection mode chosen in the Attribute bar. Click on various points and move the mouse slightly as you click, this will create a nice rounded curve. Use as much of the area as possible.
- In PhotoImpact, once you have created a basic curve, use the Path Edit tool and move the anchor points of your path until you have a suitably ribbon-like shape. In Paint Shop Pro, use the Object Selector in a similar way.
- When you have made the line, duplicate it to make the other edge of the ribbon. As a shortcut in Photoshop you can click on the selection tool with the ALT key held down, and drag out a duplicate line.
- Now join the two ends up, again in Photoshop you can do this using the Pen tool, hold down the ALT key and click on the end of one of the lines and then again on the corresponding end of the other line. Do the same at the other end.
- To turn the path into a selection, press the CTRL/⌘+ ENTER in Photoshop and SHIFT+CTRL/⌘+ B in Paint Shop Pro.
- To color the ribbon in, select the airbrush and using dark and light variations on the same colors, work your way down the ribbon. You can add a touch of dodge and burn to highlight the curves. If the lines cross unconvincingly in places, you should zoom in on the areas where this happens and manually fill in the missing bits of ribbon.
- When you have finished, use the transform tools to make the far end disappear into the distance and to angle it accordingly.
- To make more ribbons of differing colors, repeat the process.

Trick 63: Tasteful vase

To complete the effect:
- Copy and paste the Eiffel Tower picture into the vase picture, and scale it to reduce the image to the size you want it to appear on the vase.
- We now need to distort the Eiffel image slightly so that it look as though it is painted onto the vase. These tools are found under the Filter > Distort menu in Photoshop and the Effects > Geometric Effects in Paint Shop Pro. The best way to achieve the same effect in PhotoImpact is by using the Effect > Warping option. Put a slight bend into the Eiffel tower layer. You may also wish to turn the layer on its side so that you can bend the image across its width as well as lengthways. Remember to rotate it back afterwards.
- Using the polygonal lasso tool, make a selection around the right-hand side of the image (where it corresponds with the bend in the vase). Again, use the distort tools to bend the side of the image up to correspond with the shape of the vase. Do the same on the other side.
- Change the blending mode of this layer to Multiply. This should make it look like it is a part of the vase.
- Finally, use the eraser tool with a soft brush setting to rub round the edges of the image so that the leaf comes to the front and the edges of the image are blurred, as found on tasteful memorabilia adorning the window sills of aunts and grandparents the world over.

Stonehenge

Trick 64: Stonehenge Shadows

You will need:

- One picture of a mysterious ancient monument, such as Stonehenge on Salisbury Plain, UK.

To complete the effect:

1. Our first step is to create a more exotic sky. With the magic wand tool, select the sky, and all the little bits of sky in between Stonehenge's "legs".

2. Keep this area selected, and then create a linear gradient of your choice to make a nice sunset effect. This one is yellow-green, red, orange and blue from the Color Harmonies 1 palette in Photoshop Elements. The layer uses a Hue blending mode.

3. Using the lasso tool, carefully draw around the stones, then duplicate the selection and finally flip the layer so that it appears to reflect the actual Stonehenge.

4. Use the distort tools to adjust the perspective of the image, so that you drag the upside-down stones way out. in Photoshop Elements you can do this by clicking through Image > Transform > Perspective . In PhotoImpact you need to select the Transform tool and then choose Perspective mode by clicking on the Transform button in the left-hand corner of the Attribute toolbar.

5. Bring up the Hue/Saturation dialog and reduce the brightness to 0. Now you have very black shadows on the ground. Finally slip on a radial blur set to Zoom, and there you have a very atmospheric picture of the mysterious Stonehenge.

The larger stones were brought from a quarry 15 miles away from the site where Stonehenge was erected.

It is estimated that it would take 1000 men to haul one stone.

The average weight of the Stonehenge stones is 26 tons.

Trick 65: Arc de Henge

You will need:

- One picture of an ancient collection of rocks.
- A photo of a sturdy monument, such as the Arc de Triomphe.

To complete the effect:

- Cut around your Arc de Triomphe, and copy it on to your Stonehenge image.
- Position it carefully, and then reduce the opacity of its layer.
- Using the Lasso tool, cut away the areas that should be behind stones.
- To correct the color, open the Hue/Saturation dialog, and move the Hue slider around until it resembles the color of the surrounding stones. Reduce the Brightness to taste.

Trick 66: Building-block Henge

You will need:

- A picture of a well-known stone structure on Salisbury Plain, UK.
- One picture of a cheeky baby.

To complete the effect:

- Copy the baby on to the stones picture.
- Carefully delete away all the areas of the baby that need to appear behind stone.
- Create a new layer and give it a Multiply blending mode.
- Select nice bright pure colors – red, yellow, blue, green – and paint on the stones to make them seem like appealing colored blocks!

The Leaning Tower of Pisa

Trick 67: Tumbling the tower

You will need:

- One picture of the pre-plumbline Italian monument.

To complete the effect:

1. Using the Lasso tool, draw around the second tier of the tower, using the natural horizontal divides as your guideline.

2. When you have completed your selection, make a copy of it onto a new layer. This way you'll end up with each different tier of the tower on a different layer in your photo editor.

3. Repeat this process for each tier.

4. On the background layer, delete the original tiers away using the clone tool. There is a lot of flat sky to clone from in an environment as sunny as this.

5. Select your second tier layer and create a circular selection, the same width as the tower.

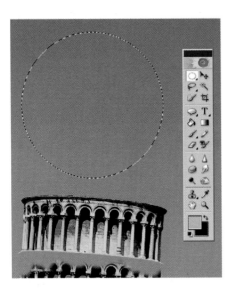

6. Select a dark stone color and a light stone color from the tower as your foreground and background colors. With the gradient tool, create a radial gradient inside the circle.

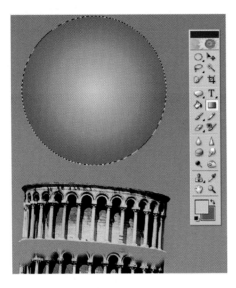

7. Using the Transform tool, move the new gradient up to the foot of the tower section you're working on, and squash it to the appropriate flatness as dictated by the perspective of the shot.

8. Repeat this process for each tier.

9. You now have a full movable sliced tower! With a move tool, arrange the tiers as you see fit – but be gentle!

The Leaning Tower of Pisa has never really been straight. It started leaning when they were building it. Nightmare!

Construction on the Leaning Tower of Pisa began on August 9th, 1173.

When the lean began, construction stopped, and only continued a century later. It then became visibly clear that the Tower of Pisa was leaning.

Because the tower tilted in different directions in its first years, it is slightly curved, like a banana.

Trick 68: Straightening the leaning tower

To complete the effect:

- Using the techniques in the previous trick, simply place the tower portions in a different position (and perhaps rotate a little).

Trick 69: One way to sort out the engineering!

To complete the effect:

- Using the marquee tool, cut out your tourist, and drag her on to a new layer.
- If necessary, flip her so she's facing away from the tower.
- Place her at the foot of the tower.
- Duplicate her layer.
- Use Hue/Saturation to make it completely dark.
- Place the layer below the original layer of the girl.
- Set its blending mode to Overlay.
- Position it as a shadow on the tower.

Easter Island

Trick 70: Easter Island garden

You will need:

- One Rano Raraku Moai from Easter Island.
- A friend or relative who Rano Raraku Moai can look down upon.

To complete the effect:

1. Using the polygonal lasso tool, cut out around your figure, and in my case, some of her foliage. Including the foliage has the added benefit of making the plants easier to blend in with the original image's grass.

2. Paste and resize the cutout image onto the Moai image in a new layer.

3. Trim around the cutout with the lasso tool and eraser to get rid of parts of the background—with the exception of the lower edge, which we'll take care of in the next couple of steps.

4. Give your lasso tool a feather of 9 to 12 pixels, and in your person layer, chose an exaggerated ragged path along the bottom of the image.

5. The feathering that we added means that when the polygonal selection is complete, the selection area will become rounded.

6. Hit DELETE. The edge will be blurry, and blends into the background fairly smoothly.

7. And there you have it: our friend's garden is a success under the watchful eye of a Rano Raraku Moai!

The first inhabitants of Easter Island came around 400 AD.

The statues weigh roughly 50 tons each.

Around 100 statues are still standing.

Most of the Easter Island statues are from 10 to 20 feet tall, but some are up to 40 feet.

Trick 71: Monolithic garden gnomes

Trick 72: Christmas on Easter Island

To complete the effect:

- Using the lasso tools and erasers, cut out the background behind the Moai.
- Cut and paste randomly into a garden in new layers; resize so that they are garden gnome size.
- Cut away parts of the garden that the gnomes are hiding behind. Create shadows if necessary, you can do this in Photoshop with the paintbrush Darken value set to 30 to 50, depending on how bright the sun is shining. In other programs, just use a soft gray brush at a fairly low opacity to create the shadows.

To complete the effect:

- Use the lasso tool to select the whole of the statue, following the edges very carefully.
- Copy the selection onto a new layer.
- Use the saturation/hue controls to remove the color from the selection.
- Fill the selection with an 80% opacity of red – this will allow the contours of the statue to show through as they would do through wrapping paper.
- Add the holly sprigs and the label using the Shape tool. If you don't have any holly shapes in your custom shape list, then add some stars instead.
- Pinch and distort the holly sprig shapes so they seem to follow the contours of the statue. Use the dodge and burn tools to create some shading and highlights.
- On a new layer add a label using the shape tool, and then use the Text tool to add some seasonal greeting. Now that is one impressive gift!

Sydney Opera House

Trick 73: Opera in space!

You will need:

- A photo of a space-age building such as Sydney Opera House.

To complete the effect:

1. Open the Sydney image and create a new layer from the background. Use the selection tools to select the building itself. A tool that looks for contrast, like the Magnetic Lasso tool, would be ideal here.

2. Invert your selection and delete the rest of the image.

3. Create a new fill layer with 100% opacity black. Place this layer behind the opera house layer.

4. Select the black layer and duplicate it. On the duplicate layer, use the elliptical selection tool to select a circular area of background and fill it with color. Apply a radial gradient to this circular area – et voila! A planet!

5. On the same layer, paint on stars using a small circular brush and dots of white color. Vary the size and opacity of these dots to give a feeling of depth to your star field.

6. Use the eraser to remove any excess white from around the opera house – the black background will make this much easier.

7. Duplicate your Opera House layer and add a motion blur to the lower layer.

8. Depending on how your software's motion blur facility works, you may now need to move the top Opera House layer so that it only has a blur appearing from one (trailing) end.

9. Merge the two layers (the Opera House and the blur).

10. As an optional final step, use the levels (or equivalent) to give the impression of a spacy kinda lighting! I used the input levels of 50, 1, and 200.

The Opera House was designed by Danish architect Jørn Utzon, and was opened in 1973.

The Opera House has an annual audience of 2 million for its performances.

There are 2194 pre-cast concrete sections making up the roof.

Originally, Utzon designed an equally radical, curvy and organic interior, but this design was not used, and a more sober interior was adopted.

Trick 74: Message in a bottle

To complete the effect:

- Use the selection tools to cut out a picture of a bottle and note.
- Copy it onto a layer above the Opera House.
- Duplicate this layer.
- On the duplicate layer, erase everything except the note and the very edge of the bottle.
- Use a gentle eraser (roughly 30% opacity) to lightly blend the inner edge of this bottle "outline".
- On the other layer, delete the note and reduce the layer opacity to 40% to allow the background to show through.
- Merge these two layers together to give you your finished bottle. Position it where you'd like it to go in the water and erase a section from the bottom to sink it into the waves.
- Use the sharpen tool to sharpen the edges of the waves where they meet the bottle.

Trick 75: Opera flowers

To complete the effect:

- Create the space effect as far as having the Opera House on a black background.
- Copy the Opera House layer, and flip the copy horizontally.
- Now rotate the opera house so that the straight edges line up with each other.
- Erase all but the 'sails' of your new layer, so that the darker area (lower floors) have disappeared.
- Move the upside-down layer a little closer to its parent.
- Use the clone tool to soften the edges between the Opera Houses (or petals).
- Merge the layers, then erase any remaining unnecessary bits, for example the lower floors of the original opera house.
- On a new layer, beneath the 'flower head', draw a stalk so it disappears beneath the flower.
- You could also (as here) color the back of the Opera House green to match the stem, and apply a different background.

The Riddle of the Sphinx

Trick 76: Cold as Ice!

You will need:

- One picture of the Sphinx.

To complete the effect:

1. Fortunately, sand is a perfect color for creating ice. Don't believe me? See how easy this one is! First select the Sphinx with the lasso tool.

2. Invert the colors. To do this, go to Image > Adjustments > Invert, in PhotoImpact you'll find this under Format > Invert, and in Paint Shop Pro you'll see that it's at Colors > Negative Image.

3. Open the Levels dialog and change the Input levels to 0, 1.0, 188. This will sharpen your sphinx up slightly.

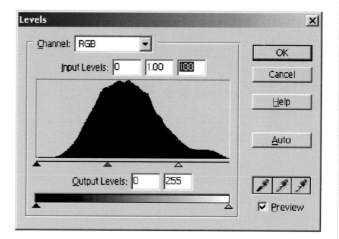

4. Now, let's make the background snowy. Select the sandy desert and the pyramid that we can see in the background and again invert the color to make a negative effect. Again we'll use a Levels adjustment, but this time we'll set the midtone marker very low, to about 4.5. You'll see your background change to a snowy landscape.

5. If you're using Photoshop Elements, open the Effects menu and select the blizzard icon; drag it on to your picture – instant blizzard! In PhotoImpact click through Effect > Creative > Particle > Snow. In my example I've also added a cloud effect from the same menu.

6. And there we have it - a Sphinx cast in ice!

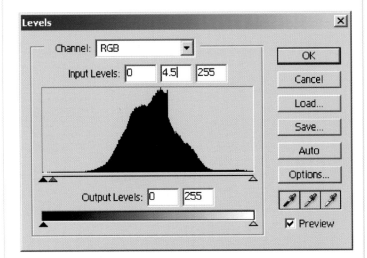

The Sphinx is a mythical creature that was built around 4500 years ago.

It is the largest single monolithic statue in the world.

In the 15th century, Muslim troops broke off the nose of the Great Sphinx because their religion forbids the image of gods.

The statue is 200 feet long and 65 feet high.

The sphinx is built of soft sandstone and would have disappeared long ago had it not been buried in sand for so long. Time is short, so don't expect to see it for much longer!

Trick 77: Sphinx carving

To complete the effect:

Nevertheless, in case you were wondering, here's how to carve writing into the side of the Sphinx.

- Select the type tool and type in the words you want – you can easily position and resize the writing against the picture as you go. Make sure that the type color is white.
- In Photoshop Elements, open the Layers Styles palette and choose a simple Inner Shadow.
- Then add a simple Inner Glow, make sure that the color of the glow is black or dark gray. If you have the option of changing the blending mode and the opacity of the Inner Glow, then set the blending mode to Multiply and the opacity to about 40%.
- Select the type layer and on the layers palette, change the layer to Multiply. Select the type area by CTRL/⌘+clicking on the layer in the Layers palette.
- Go to the original background layer and lower the brightness and saturation.

Trick 78: Moonlit Sphinx

To complete the effect:

- Duplicate the background layer. Call this layer Night.
- Cut around the outline of the Sphinx precisely, and copy and paste this into a new layer. Call the new layer Cutout.
- Select the Night layer and adjust the Hue/Saturation until the background is suitably dark.
- Now we'll add some atmospheric lighting to the Sphinx. Select the Cutout layer. In Photoshop choose Filter > Render > Lighting Effects, and in Paint Shop Pro go to Effects > Illumination Effects. Choose a Spotlight, if available go for a triple spotlight so you have lots of spots to play with!
- Now manipulate each of the spots in terms of direction and breadth of field on the preview image. I have chosen to move them around so that the light source is coming from below rather than above. You can also adjust sliders for Intensity and Focus. By manipulating each spot this way you can light up the Sphinx. When you are happy, click OK. If you do not like the outcome, go to Edit > Undo and try again.
- Select the Night layer. Again add some lighting effects, this time select an Omni light. In PhotoImpact you don't have this option, so instead choose a Flashlight and adjust the brightness setting so that it is relatively low. Adjust the light until you're happy and then click OK.
- Finally, add a few stars: Select the airbrush, choose a soft-edged brush and adjust the pressure to about 20%.

Monument Valley

Trick 79: Desert conveniences

You will need:

- One serene desert scene.
- One convenience (or set thereof).

To complete the effect:

1. Draw around the toilet and bidet, using the polygonal selection tool.

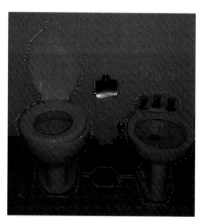

2. Copy and paste them into your serene background as a new layer. Resize if necessary.

3. Select and delete any of the bad edges, using your eraser.

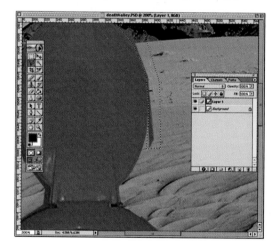

4. Make a copy of the toilet layer and put it behind the original toilet image layer. Flip the layer copy vertically, and drag it to match the bottom of the original layer.

5. Now to make some shadows. Use the Transform tools to stretch the layer copy in the direction of other shadows in the image. When transforming two items like this, it's best to select and transform each one separately. Erase any part of the image that wouldn't show as a shadow, such as the bottom edge of the bidet.

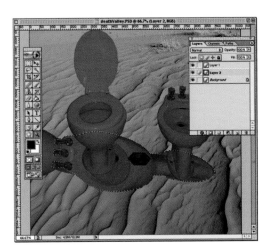

6. With this shadow layer outline selected, hide this layer and make the background layer active. Feather the selection so that the edges of the shadow will be slightly blurred. Experiment with this amount to find the best effect.

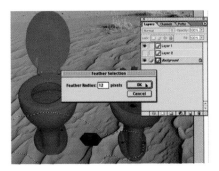

7. Now fill the outline with black at a low opacity and set the blending mode to darken. In Photoshop, it's easy to do this by going to Edit > Fill. In all other programs use the Paint bucket option to fill the area.

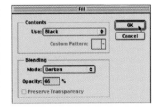

8. Using the paintbrush, use black and white at a low opacity to paint in shadows and highlight. In this case, since the sun is coming from the right side of the image, we lightened edges on that side, and darkened them on the other. Where the bidet's shadow might hit the toilet, we also made it darker. If you're feeling adventurous try adding some sand blowing over the edges of the bottom part of the toilets with the Clone tool.

And here you have it, convenience right in the middle of the desert! It could only happen in California!

Monument Valley is a Navajo Tribal Park, owned and operated by the Navajo people.

Prolonged drought in the Valley has seen many of the Navajo people leave the area.

The Valley is known to be the place where movie director John Ford filmed his most famous Westerns. Directors of Westerns are now widely thought to avoid using Monument Valley because Ford made it so completely his own.

Trick 80: Monument valley road signs

You will need:

- One picture of the desert.
- A road sign.

To complete the effect:

- Pick any sort of traffic signal or sign.
- Using the same techniques as above, place the sign in the sand, make a shadow with an outline of a copy of the original. Remember to feather the outline so that the shadow doesn't have hard edges.
- Select and delete areas that should be behind sand.

Trick 81: Hand-drawn desert sunset

You will need:

- One image of a desert with a beautiful sunset.
- A picture of a hand holding a pen.

To complete the effect:

- Using the distort tools, alter the shape of the desert, so it looks like it is lying flat.
- Duplicate the sunset layer and if you have a Find Edges filter apply this now. Then desaturate the color of this layer.
- Enhance the lines by using the Levels command. The idea is that the edges should start to disappear from the sky. Slide the far left slider towards the middle until the lines start to darken.
- Select the eraser tool and reduce its opacity to around 45%. Begin erasing the layer with the lines on it so that the color photograph of the desert begins to show through.
- Open your hand image and use the lasso tool to make a selection around the hand and the pen. Copy and paste this into the desert image.
- Create a new layer under the hand layer. On this layer add shadows using the burn tool or a soft black paint at low opacity. Use the move tool until the shadows are in position and add a Gaussian blur of around 20%.
- Activate the hand layer, and using the eraser tool with a soft edge and an opacity of around 45%, erase the back end of the hand so it looks like it's fading in.
- Create another new layer and fill it with white, and move it to the bottom of the Layers palette, you now have the hand emerging from a blank page.

Taj Mahal

Trick 82: Dolphins at the Taj Mahal

You will need:
- A mystical monument.
- A mysterious beast of the sea.

To complete the effect:

1. Select the dolphin using an appropriate selection tool, perhaps the Magnetic Lasso or equivalent.

2. To copy the selected area go to the EDIT menu and choose COPY.

3. Paste your selection onto the Taj Mahal image – notice that a new layer has been created in the layer palette, rename this layer as 'dolphin.'

4. Using the move tool, reposition the dolphin until you feel that it is correctly placed and, if required, tidy the edges using the eraser tool.

5. To make the dolphin appear more realistic in its new surroundings, there are a couple of effects that you can apply. Firstly you can alter the 'brightness and contrast' using whichever tool your software allows.

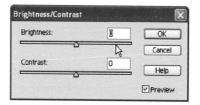

6. In some applications you can alternatively apply "rendered" effects (In Photoshop from the Filter > Render > submenu, in Paint Shop Pro from the Effects > Illumination > submenu.

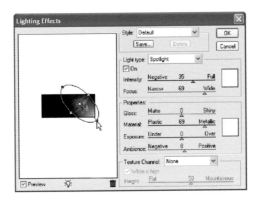

7. Using the Paintbrush tool with white as the foreground colour create a spray effect between the water and the dolphin (I have used various sized spatter brushes and altered the opacity of the colour to 80%).

8. Select the pond using an appropriate tool (Polygonal Lasso, for example) and apply a suitable water ripple effect.

9. With some more advanced programs, you could also add wave-like ripples by copying the pond onto another layer above, then applying an inverted Spherize filter to it and finally erasing arcs to give an impression of ripples spreading outwards.

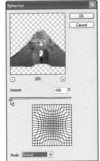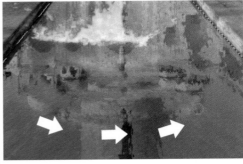

10. Finally, make reflections of the Dolphin and Spray layers by copying each layer, then applying the flip function to the layer. (In Photoshop Elements, this is confusingly found under Image > Rotate > Flip Layer Vertical, in Paint Shop Pro Image > Flip)

11. Reduce the opacity of the flipped reflections and apply a ripple filter to them both.

It is forbidden for aircraft to fly over the Taj Mahal.

The Taj Mahal was actually built for use as a tomb.

It is believed that another Taj Mahal was supposed to be built in black marble, opposite the existing one, and for the two to be connected by a bridge.

The Taj Mahal was once scheduled to be torn down in the 1830's.

Trick 83: The city behind the Taj Mahal

Trick 84: A Towerless Taj Mahal

To complete the effect:

- Copy the 'background' layer of your Taj Mahal.
- On the new layer, select and delete the area behind the temple, perhaps using the Magic Wand tool.
- Copy your background image, placing it between the original Taj Mahal 'background' layer and the copied layer without a sky. Position it to one side of the layer.
- Copy that layer, and flip it along the horizontal.
- Merge the two new cityscape layers, then copy the new layer and flip it vertically.
- Using a selection tool delete all of the reflected layer except the pool surface. (You can make this easier by temporarily reducing the opacity to see the shape of the pool).
- Finally dull down the Brightness and Contrast of that layer.

To complete the effect:

- Select the Clone Stamp tool (or equivalent), then carefully cover the towers with the sky until they disappear.
- Use varied brush sizes to create an accurate effect.

The Pyramids

Trick 85: Faye rebuilds the Pyramids

You will need:

- An image of the Pyramids, or another wonder of the ancient world.

- A picture of the beach.

To complete the effect:

1. Open both images in your editing program.

2. Using the Rectangular Marquee tool, select around the pyramids. Don't worry about being too exact as we're just going to copy the rectangle straight over.

3. Paste your pyramids as a new layer over your background.

4. Scale and position your monument in an appropriate place on your beach. Here we're going to put the bottom of the pyramids near that area of messy sand on the left.

5. Working on the pyramid layer, select and delete the background – use the magic wand or equivalent – and tidy up the edges with the eraser tool.

6. Because we have combined two completely unrelated images the shadows are positioned in different directions. In this case all we need to do is flip the pyramids horizontally.

7. If necessary, reposition and erase again.

8. For that just-built effect, use the clone stamp (or equivalent) to add some random piles of sand to the bottom of the pyramids.

9. Soften or blur the pyramids slightly so that they appear to match the focus of the rest of the image.

10. Finally, using a dark brush or the burn tool, paint a shadow so that the pyramids look like they've been there all along.

The pyramids used to be covered in a smooth, bright casing of small stones, which were quarried away in the 15th Century, leaving the familiar stepped look that exists today.

The Great Pyramid is the only remaining Wonder of the Ancient World.

The Great Pyramid was once the highest building on earth, and was only overtaken by the Eiffel Tower in Paris, France.

The Pyramid contains a huge scar on one side, which was caused by a British explorer trying to blast his way in during the 19th Century.

Trick 86: Pyramid's oasis

To complete the effect:

- Make a rough selection – rectangular will do – around the pyramids.
- Copy them onto a new layer.
- Flip the new layer vertically.
- Reposition the reflection to the appropriate position.
- Add an Inner Shadow layer effect (Photoshop only), then flatten the layer.
- Apply a water-like ripple effect to the layer.
- Change the opacity in the layers palette, to give the 'water' an opaque effect.
- Using the Clone Stamp tool, create a bank to the lake in front of the pyramids.

Trick 87: A little more architectural complication

To complete the effect:

This works in a very similar manner to trick 85 above, but when you insert your cutout there are some additional steps:

- Create a Hue/Saturation Adjustment Layer and group it with the Taj Mahal layer. Use this to set the Hue and Saturation values to the same as the sand.
- Attach a Levels Adjustment Layer as well, and adjust accordingly to exaggerate the shadows.
- Apply a Grainy filter, then a soft Gaussian Blur to the Taj Mahal layer.
- Make a copy of your building layer, and place it on the layer below.
- Darken that copied building so it appears completely black, then distort it so it forms a shadow shape.
- Adjust the shadow's opacity so that the ground is still visible beneath it.
- Use the same eraser and cone stamp tricks to tidy things up. Pay careful attention to which layer you're working on.

Route 66

Trick 88: Due to a terrible miscalculation of scale...

You will need:

- One picture of a nation's favorite road, with yellow lines.
- One picture of a giant wandering child.

To complete the effect:

1. Select yellow lines using magic wand tool at 32 tolerance.

2. Copy the isolated lines onto a new layer, where they can be edited separately.

3. Flip the new layer horizontal, and position the lines so they rise into the air.

4. Using the clone stamp tool, delete the original yellow lines from the background layer.

5. Place the child on the road in the crook of the yellow lines, and delete away the distant lines with the eraser.

6. From the layer with the isolated lines, copy the "straight" portion of yellow lines.

7. Paste them onto a new layer a little further up.

8. Using a perspective adjustment, set the lines to travel off into the distance. You may also need to rotate it a little.

9. Finish off with details. Delete the yellow lines that would be behind the child. Delete along the edges to taste, to get rid of any unsightly jagged parts. Use the burn tool to create shadows on the lines wrapped around the child.

10. Using the magic wand, select the left-hand yellow line and transform/drag it up against the child so that the lines come together around her torso (in elastic style).

Route 66 was only paved end to end in 1937

The route is 4000 km long.

The road was designed in 1926, picking up as many bits and pieces of existing road as possible.

The road crosses eight states and three time-zones.

Route 66 is also know as "The Mother Road", "The Main Street of America" and as "The Will Rogers Highway".

Trick 89: River 66

To complete this effect:

- Create a new layer from the background.
- Use the magic wand tool to select the whole of the road surface.
- Cut away all this area.
- Copy an image of a rushing river onto a new layer – place this layer behind the Route 66 layer and use the move tool to position it appropriately.
- Use the eraser tool to erase any problematic overlapping.
- Use the blur tool to soften the edges where the banks meet the river.

Trick 90: Beam me up!!

To complete this effect:

- Use a combination of the rectangular and elliptical marquee selection tools to select the area that will form the 'beam'.
- Adjust the brightness of this layer to make it much brighter than the rest of the image.
- With the beam still selected, apply a diffuse glow filter.
- Use the 'select inverse' option to select the rest of the image and reduce the brightness to make it look like night-time (everyone knows that all UFO abductions happen at night).
- Copy and paste on the poor schmuck getting sucked up into the UFO.
- Apply a motion blur to him to suggest upward movement.

Niagara Falls

Trick 91: Rainbow

You will need:

- An awesome landscape, such as Niagara Falls.

To complete this effect:

1. Start out by adding a delicious lens flare (Photoshop: Filter > Render > Lens Flare; Paint Shop Pro: Effects > Illumination Effects > sunburst; PhotoImpact Effects > Creative > Lighting). Then position it over the falls.

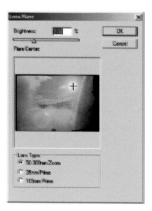

2. Create a new layer and call it Rainbow. In Photoshop, select the gradient tool and set it to Radial. (In Paint Shop Pro, click the Styles box to bring up the Gradient dialog, and set it to Sunburst).

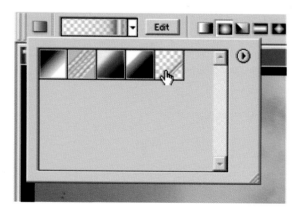

3. Photoshop Elements: in the gradient palette go to Special Effects, and choose Russell's Rainbow (Photoshop Elements only). Using the center of one of the dots of your existing lens flare as a starting point, drag out a gradient line. When you release the mouse button, a rainbow will appear.

4. Paint Shop Pro: select the Marquee tool; set it to draw a circular marquee. Using the center of one of the dots of your existing lens flare as a starting point, drag out a circular marquee.

5. Set the Layer Blending Mode to Overlay, and reduce the opacity to 50%.

6. We need to blur our rainbow. Use the marquee tool to draw a box around the circular rainbow, leaving a small gap on each side for the blur to bed in.

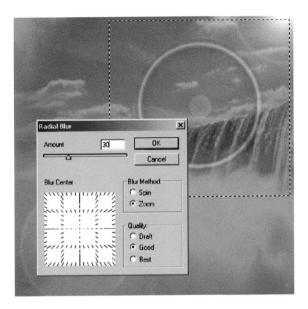

7. Add a radial blur and set it to 30. There we have it!

Around one fifth of the world's fresh water lies in the Great Lakes, and most of it flows over Niagara Falls. Shaken, not stirred!

High wire tightrope acts used to walk across the river – but they don't let 'em do it now!

The first person to go over the falls in a barrel and survive was a 63-year-old female schoolteacher.

Trick 92: Alien Niagara

To complete the effect:

- In Photoshop, add a Gradient Map Adjustment layer. Apply a violet/orange gradient from the default palette.
- Change the layer blending mode to Overlay.
- With the magic wand tool set to a Tolerance of 10, select the sky, leaving the clouds and waterfall unselected.
- Create a new layer.
- Select the gradient tool. With a Yellow, Violet, Orange, Blue gradient selected (it's in the default palette), draw out a gradient across the sky.
- Set the layer blending mode to Soft Light.
- Make a new layer and dot the sky with white dots of varying sizes. Set the layer mode to Screen. Now we have a universe!

Trick 93: Extreme diving

To complete the effect:

- Draw around the girl using the lasso tool.
- Copy and paste her on to the Niagara image.
- Transform her scale to suit the picture. Apply a motion blur and set it to around 20, with an angle in the direction of the figure's fall.
- On a new layer, use a large white paintbrush at a low opacity to paint in waterfall spray!

Grand Canyon

Trick 94: Grand Canyon waterfall

You will need:

- One photograph of the Grand Canyon.
- One photograph of a waterfall.

To complete the effect:

We are going to alter the landscape of the Grand Canyon, add a waterfall, making it all blend in together, and finally change the color.

1. Open the file and use the Lasso Tool (Freehand Tool in Paint Shop Pro) to draw a rough selection around the rocks on the left-hand side.

2. Copy and paste this selection into a new layer. In Photoshop you could use a handy shortcut to do this. CTRL/⌘+J. Turn off the background layer by clicking on the Eye icon in the Layers Palette (the glasses in Paint Shop Pro). You should now only see the layer you have just created.

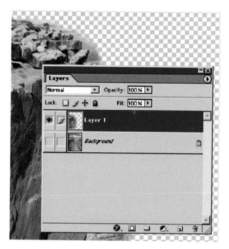

3. Now flip the new layer horizontally, by going into Edit > Transform > Flip Horizontal for Photoshop users, Image > Mirror for those using Paint Shop Pro, Edit > Rotate and Flip > Flip Horizontally in PhotoImpact, and Format > Flip > Selected Object > Horizontally in Picture It!

4. Using the Move tool, slide the rock layer over to the right - hand side of the screen. Zoom close into the rocks, and using a combination of the lasso tool and eraser tool with a small soft-edged-brush, remove the background around the rocks.

5. Keep erasing until you're left with just the rocks. Here's a great tip for Paint Shop Pro users – if you erase too much then click the right mouse button, or hit CTRL on a Mac to bring the erased areas back. In any other program, remember you can always go to Edit > Undo to correct a mistake. The shortcut for this is CTRL/⌘+2.

6. Turn on the visibility of the background layer by again. If necessary, use the move tool and cursor keys to nudge the rock layer to line it up with the original background layer.

7. With the rocks now forming the basis for the water to flow down, we can now add the waterfall. Open the waterfall picture. Create a rough selection around the main waterfall and copy it to the clipboard.

8. Switch back to our newly formed rock scene, and paste the waterfall into a new layer. Scale and stretch the waterfall so that it fits between the rocks, with the top of the water coming over the top of the rocks, like the sample here.

9. Using a medium-sized soft-edge eraser, remove the unwanted rocks from the waterfall image.

10. Using the brightness and contrast and levels commands, alter the background layer until it fits nicely with the waterfall. Adjust the waterfall if needed.

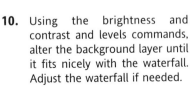

The Grand Canyon National Park includes over a million acres of land.

Grand Canyon is 277 miles long.

The width of the canyon varies between 10 and 18 miles

Depthwise, it's over a vertical mile from the edge of the rim to the river below.

Trick 95: Old time Waterfall Canyon

To complete the effect:

- Take your image from the previous trick and flatten the image so all layers become one. Photoshop users, go to Layers > Flatten Image, if you're using Paint Shop Pro go to Layers > Merge > Merge All, and PhotoImpact users will find this command under Object > Merge All.
- You cannot merge the layers in Picture It! so you will have to adjust each layer separately, or you could simply go to Effects > Antique for an immediate sepia tone effect!
- We now want to remove the color from the image, in Photoshop you can use a handy shortcut, CTRL/⌘+SHIFT+U. In other programs, simply reduce the saturation down as far as it will go in the Hue/Saturation dialog box.
- Now, let's add a sepia tone. You need to go back to the Hue/Saturation dialog box, and check the Colorize box. In most programs you can create a sepia tone by setting both the Hue and Saturation levels to approximately 30, but you will need to experiment until you find a good tone. In PhotoImpact you need to set the Hue to about −135, and the Saturation to −35 with the Lightness set to 10.
- To make the picture look aged, you could add a little noise and scratches via a noise filter, which you'll find under the Effects or Filters menu.
- As a final touch, add a faded border to give it a really old-fashioned feel. You may have ready-made borders available in your program, but if not you can create your own. First make a new layer under your waterfall layer and fill with white. In the waterfall layer, make a rectangular selection around the edge of the image, with about 30 pixels of feathering, invert the selection and then hit DELETE. And there you have it – modern technology has helped you to create an image that you could have made a hundred years ago with a box, a pin and a few chemicals!!

Trick 96: Mars Canyon

You will need:

- A picture of the Grand Canyon.
- One image of an astronaut (this one comes courtesy of the NASA image exchange at http://nix.nasa.gov).

To complete the effect:

- First, in your Grand Canyon image make a selection around the sky and delete it.
- Now add a Hue/Saturation adjustment to emphasize the red colors in the image, making the craggy rocks appear to come from the Red Planet.
- Make a red linear gradient and place this in a new layer to make a spacy sky.
- Use the lasso/freehand tools to make a selection around your astronaut and paste him into your canyon image, scale him as necessary.
- Cover any existing reflections in your astronaut's helmet using the clone stamp tool, and add additional highlights using a small brush with white paint, then create a new reflection using the colors of the background layer. And there you have it – zero gravity in the Martian Grand Canyon.

The Pont du Gard

Trick 97: Out of bounds

You will need:

- A photo of the Pont du Gard or another aqueduct.

To complete the effect:

1. Open the bridge image and duplicate the image onto a new layer. On this layer, use the rectangular marquee selection tool to draw a large rectangle and fill it with a wood-grain pattern.

2. Use the rectangular marquee selection again to draw another rectangle within this one and delete it, leaving a frame

3. To give the frame a degree of three-dimensionality, use the polygonal marquee selection tool to select the top and bottom edges (complete with diagonal join in the corner in the style of a picture frame) and reduce the brightness of these selections by about 60%.

4. Still on the frame layer, use the eraser to remove all the portions of the frame which would be behind the bridge.

5. Merge the two layers together and then use the various selection tools to select and delete everything except the frame and the portion of bridge that sticks out of it.

6. Create a new fill layer, filled with solid white color, and place it behind the framed bridge.

7. Now we just need to give the framed bridge its shadow. Select the framed bridge layer and duplicate it. On the new layer, reduce the brightness and contrast till it turns solid black. Reduce the opacity to 75% and apply a blur filter to 'fuzz' the edges. Finally, offset slightly against the framed bridge itself, and we have our shadow.

8. The only thing that looks wrong is the area near the top right where the frame is visible through one of the arches – the stonework should be casting a shadow on the frame. Use the lasso tool to select a small portion of the stonework to the left of that arch and copy it onto a new layer, which you place above all the others.

9. Convert to shadow as in step 7. Position the shape so that the shadow falls onto the frame (you may need to erase some of the shadow if it overlaps the stonework after being repositioned).

The Pont du Gard is a Roman aqueduct located in Nimes in Southern France.

This section was part of an aqueduct nearly 30 miles long which supplied Nimes with water.

The structure dates back to around the 15th century BC.

On its first level, the Pont du Gard carries a road and, at the top of the third level, a water channel.

Trick 98: Stay in lane

To complete the effect:

- Create a new layer above the main image.
- On this layer, use the shape tool to draw a rectangle with feathered corners and fill it with white color.
- On top of this draw another rectangle, this time filled green. Line them up so as to have a green rectangle with a white border.
- Use the shape tool to draw three shields and three arrows and position them within the rectangle.
- Use a text tool to write on the appropriate traffic direction text.
- Merge all layers except the background.
- Use the skew and perspective tools to alter the shape of your sign such that it looks as if it is fixed to the bridge.
- Copy the sign onto a new layer, reduce the brightness and contrast until it appears black. Reduce the opacity to 75%, blur it a bit, and offset it slightly from the sign to form the sign's shadow.

Trick 99: Bridge from the Moon to the Earth

To complete the effect:

- Open the bridge image and also an image of the Earth.
- Use the selection tools to cut out the bridge and paste it onto a new layer above the earth.
- Use the eraser to remove all remaining background from around the bridge, including any visible through the archways
- Use the blur tool to blur the join between the bridge and the earth's cloud cover, to give the impression of the bridge disappearing into the clouds.
- As an optional final step, merge the layers and use the levels (or equivalent) to give the impression of a spacey kind of lighting! I used the input levels of 50, 1, and 200.
- And now you have a sturdy bridge to take you from the Moon to the Earth – if only NASA had thought of that!

DESIGNER TO DESIGNER™

Registration Code: 42832V1J5D9T5VR01

friends of ED writes books for you. Any suggestions, or ideas about how you want information given in your ideal book will be studied by our team.

Your comments are valued by friends of ED.

For technical support please contact support@friendsofed.com.

Freephone in USA   800.873.9769
Fax   312.893.8001
UK contact: Tel: 0121.687.4100
Fax: 0121.687.4101

99 Phenomenal Digital Photo Tricks: *Crazy fun with people & places*

Name ....

Address ....

City .... State/Region ....

Country .... Postcode/Zip ....

E-mail ....

Profession: design student ☐   freelance designer ☐

amateur photographer ☐   professional photographer ☐

other (please specify) ....

Age: Under 20 ☐ 20-24 ☐ 25-29 ☐ 30-40 ☐ over 40 ☐

Do you use: mac ☐ pc ☐ both ☐

How did you hear about this book?..

Book review (name)..

Advertisement (name)...

Recommendation ....

Catalog ....

Other ....

Where did you buy this book? Bookstore (name) ....

City.................................Computer Store (name)...........................

Mail Order.......................Other..................................

How did you rate the overall content of this book?

Excellent ☐   Good ☐

Average ☐   Poor ☐

What applications/technologies do you intend to learn in the near future?...............

....

What did you find most useful about this book? ....

....

What did you find the least useful about this book? ....

....

Please add any additional comments ....

....

What other subjects will you buy a computer book on soon?

....

What is the best computer book you have used this year?

....

Note: This information will only be used to keep you

updated about new friends of ED titles and will not be used for any other purpose or

passed to any other third party.

friendsof

DESIGNER TO DESIGNER™

NB. If you post the bounce back card below in the UK, please send it to:

friends of ED Ltd.,
1102 Arden House,
Warwick Road,
Acocks Green,
Birmingham.
B27 6BH.

BUSINESS REPLY MAIL
FIRST CLASS   PERMIT #64   CHICAGO, IL

POSTAGE WILL BE PAID BY ADDRESSEE

**friends of ED,
29 S. La Salle St.
Suite 520
Chicago Il 60603-USA**